Tea Explorations Journal

Track Your Own Tea Tasting Adventures

Alan & Marlys Arnold

This Journal belongs to:

Dated from: to:

Tiffany Harbor Productions

Published by Tiffany Harbor Productions in 2016
First edition

www.AdventureswithTea.com

Cover background image and interior images from Digital Juice, except for clipper ship image on page 98 from Wikimedia Commons

ISBN 978-0-9712905-5-6

Quantity discounts are available on bulk purchases of this book for reselling, educational purposes, subscription incentives, gifts or fundraising. For more information, please contact Tiffany Harbor Productions, PO Box 901808, Kansas City, MO 64190-1808

Dedication

To lovers of tea at every level of experience
who long for the next adventure
and to our *Adventures with Tea* fans
who have shared the journey with us

How to Use this Journal

Why Keep a Tea Journal?

While tea has been a favored drink around the world for centuries, it is also a very personal experience. Even when you're enjoying tea with friends, each of you may walk away with your own impressions and memories.

This book was designed to provide you a place to keep all your tea tasting experiences organized in one place. Whether you're a long-time tea enthusiast or just beginning to discover the world's second-most consumed beverage, you can use this journal to record your own personal reflections on the attributes of teas, as well as your overall tasting experience (the atmosphere, company you're with, etc.).

Many people say they don't like tea, and that could be due to unpleasant past experiences. Many of those are probably due to either bad or inferior teas. When you are willing to try new flavors, you may find some you don't like. But you'll most certainly also discover ones you can't believe you've been living without.

Above all, don't be intimidated. You don't have to do a formal tea cupping or Chinese gong fu ceremony. Simply brew, pour, and savor the teas you've chosen. Then use this journal as a way to record your explorations.

Here are some suggestions to make the most out of this book:

1. Use the fill-in-the-blank **Table of Contents** to keep track of each tea experience so you can easily find the ones you want later.
2. In the **At-Home Experiences** section, record the teas you brew in your own kitchen. Write down the flavor, brand and where you purchased each tea, along with notes about brewing details and who is joining you that day. Then use the notes section to express your thoughts about the tea's taste, aroma, and your overall impression. (See the following pages for some tasting note ideas, and a sample form filled out.)

3. The **Out & About Experiences** section is designed for you to use both in your hometown or when you're traveling. Here you'll record much of the same details about the actual tea. In addition, there are several ways to rate the venue where you're enjoying the tea, as well as an area for you to attach the venue's business card for later reference. (See the following section for a sample form filled out.) You could even include any thoughts, sketches or doodles that are sparked by the experience!

4. This book is more than just a journal. You'll also discover nuggets of tea history, tips and trivia, including an extensive timeline of tea-related world events on pages 62-63. There are even a couple of word puzzles for you to work on while sipping your tea.

5. In the back of the book, you'll find lists for recording places you want to visit, teas you'd like to try, and people to share them with.

Above all, have fun with this book and add your own creative elements. Journal by yourself or with family members or friends. By creating your own personal tea tasting history, you'll have a keepsake for the future.

ALAN & MARLYS

Want a creative bookmark for your journal?

Get a free sheet of printable full-color bookmarks for all your tea-related reading!

Visit: www.AdventureswithTea.com/myjournal

Tea Tasting Notes

You've likely been drinking tea for years, or at least have tasted it multiple times throughout your lifetime. But how often have you stopped to consider the complexity of what you're drinking? (We're talking quality tea here ... not the run-of-the-mill kind you find on supermarket shelves. If that's what you think of when we say tea, we challenge you to go way beyond that to explore the world of options that awaits you.)

Tea is like wine or cheese – each one you taste has its own unique characteristics, depending on the environment it came from and how it was processed.

If you've never analyzed a tea (or any other food) before, some of these terms may seem a bit strange. But trust us ... it will make sense as you begin to fill out the notes in your journal.

What to consider

Appearance, aroma, flavor, mouthfeel – the Chinese have been studying these characteristics of tea for centuries in their tea ceremonies.

Appearance

First, pay attention to the appearance of both the leaves and the brewed infusion. What colors do you see? (Is it yellow, yellow-green, green, amber, red, dark brown, black or something else?)

Aroma

Smell before you taste (and even before brewing if possible). Is the aroma faint, medium or strong?

In order to get the full aroma of the tea, lean in and breathe deeply. What does it smell like? Does it remind you of something or transport your mind somewhere? Do the leaves smell like the brewed infusion, or are they different?

Start with broad descriptions (earthy), then narrow it down (hay/straw). Use the Tea Aroma & Taste Vocabulary Chart at the end of these tasting notes, but don't be confined by these terms. Perhaps the best description for you would be "reminiscent of a savory mushroom broth."

Flavor

Aroma and taste are closely related. In fact, a majority of what we taste is actually what we are smelling - up to 90 percent - according to sensory research. Our taste buds can isolate five major tastes: sweet, salty, sour, bitter and umami (Japanese for savory).

In an authentic tea tasting, tasters slurp the tea in and swish it around in their mouth a bit before swallowing, allowing the liquid to pass over all the taste buds. (Of course official tea tasters also spit out the tea, but we don't necessarily advise that ... especially if you're enjoying the taste or if you're in a public place!)

Taste often comes in layers. For example, there might be an initial bright or sweet taste, followed by a more mellow aftertaste. Or it might start with a hint of floral and end with a brisk minty finish.

What is the first taste you detect? What taste comes later? Are the tastes delicate or bold? Does it remind you of something? Does any part of the taste linger? What is the texture of the tea on your tongue? Describe how the tea makes you feel or other sensations you experience as you drink the tea.

Mouthfeel

This may be a new term for you. But in the culinary world, it's used to describe how a food actually feels: the texture and consistency. For example, skim milk has a completely different feel from heavy cream, and orange juice is entirely different than soda. And if you've ever been puzzled to hear the word "dry" to describe a beverage, that means it's astringent, acidic or not sweet. In the same way, various teas can create different sensations in your mouth. Is it velvety smooth or crisp and dry?

Getting the full experience of a tea requires focus. In order to discover all the characteristics, you'll need to shut off all those thoughts racing through your mind. Get in sync with each of your senses and the messages you're receiving from the tea.

Remember there are no "right" answers. Each person's taste buds are unique, so two people may describe the same tea very differently – and that's completely okay. Your tasting experience can also be a reflection of your life experience. Tasting a flavor that reminds you of childhood days at grandma's house may bring back wonderful memories, while another flavor may remind you of a very unpleasant experience, like doing chores in the barnyard.

Learning to decode all the nuances of a good tea is great training to become more fully aware of other aspects of life and the sensory riches all around us.

What is a good tea? When you taste it, trust us, you'll know.

So relax and enjoy the adventure!

Tea Aroma & Taste Vocabulary	
Fruity	Apple, berry, citrus, grape, melon, pomegranate, stone fruit (apricot, cherry, peach, plum, etc.), tropical fruit (pineapple, mango, papaya, passion fruit, coconut, etc.)
Floral	Chamomile, gardenia, hibiscus, honeysuckle, jasmine, lavender, orange blossom, osmanthus, rose
Plants & herbs	Alfalfa, bamboo, basil, fresh cut grass, green beans, mint, parsley, spinach, squash, thyme, vegetal
Earthy	Bark, cedar, dusty, hay/straw, mossy, leather, pine, wet earth, woodsy
Savory	Bacon, brothy, burnt, buttery, smoky, toasted
Spicy	Cinnamon, cloves, ginger, nutmeg, pepper, star anise
Grain	Barley, malty
Nutty	Almond, cashew, hazelnut, peanut, pecan, walnut
Chocolate	Sweet, dark or bittersweet
Sweet	Caramel, cream, honey, marshmallow, maple syrup, molasses, toffee, vanilla

At-Home Experiences

Tea Flavor Morning in the Mountains

Date 9/5/16

Brand Adventures with Tea

Purchased from AWT website

Price ________ Today's Weather sunny

Brewing Details as directed

Who I am with Suzy from next door

Tea Type: Black, Green, Oolong, White, **Herbal**, Rooibos, Other

Appearance/Color:

Yellow Yellow–green Green Amber **Red** Dark brown Black Other

Aroma:

Floral Fruity **Citrus** Smoky Earthy Grassy Spicy Nutty Chocolate

Faint **Moderate** Strong Other Minty

Taste:

Floral **Fruity** **Citrus** Smoky Earthy Grassy Spicy Nutty Chocolate

Plant/herb Savory Malty Other Minty

Delicate Mild Flat Crisp Tangy/tart Sweet **Strong**

Mouthfeel:

Silky **Smooth** Brothy Oily Velvety Tingly **Brisk** Dry Other

My Rating (5 s = best): 4

Notes

Love the color!

Tastes like a journey into summer with fresh-picked berries

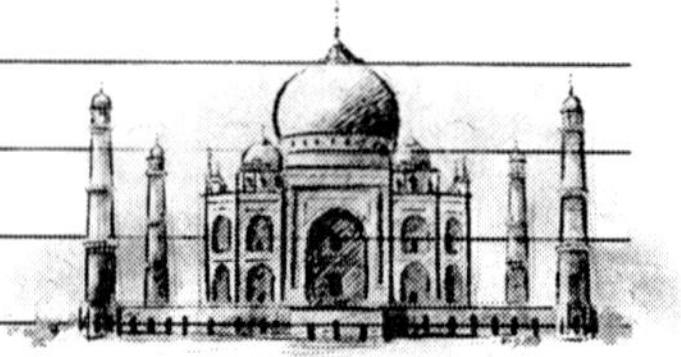

Out & About Experiences

Tea Flavor Chocolate Chai   Date 12/19/16

Venue Old Town Tea Shop   Tea Type: **Black** Green Oolong White Herbal Rooibos Other

Price $3.25   Today's Weather cold w/ hint of snow

Who I am with hubby

My Rating (5 s = best):

Venue

Staff

Tea

Food N/A

Experience

Appearance/Color:

Yellow Yellow-green Green Amber Red **Dark brown** Black Other

Aroma:

Floral Fruity Citrus Smoky Earthy Grassy **Spicy** Nutty **Chocolate**

Faint Moderate **Strong**   Other Cardamom

Taste:

Floral Fruity Citrus Smoky Earthy Grassy **Spicy** Nutty **Chocolate**

Plant/herb Savory **Malty** Other

Delicate Mild Flat Crisp Tangy/tart Sweet **Strong**

Mouthfeel:

Silky Smooth Brothy Oily **Velvety** Tingly Brisk Dry **Other** Creamy

Notes (or attach a business card or memento)

Great for a night by the fireplace!
Makes me want to go for a sleigh ride

The 7 Rules of Tea

1. Make a delicious bowl of tea.

2. Lay the charcoal so the water boils.

3. Arrange the flowers as they are in the field.

4. In summer, evoke coolness; in winter, warmth.

5. Anticipate and do everything ahead of time.

6. Prepare for rain.

7. Show every consideration for your guests.

~ Sen Rikyu, 16th Century Japanese Tea Master
on Chado (the Way of Tea)

Table of Contents

Fill in these blanks with teas and places reviewed for easy reference in the future!

At-Home Experiences

Out & About Experiences

74 ______________________________

75 ______________________________

76 Who Was Earl Grey?

77 ______________________________

78 ______________________________

79 ______________________________

80 ______________________________

81 ______________________________

82 A History of Afternoon Tea

83 ______________________________

84 ______________________________

85 ______________________________

86 ______________________________

87 ______________________________

88 ______________________________

89 ______________________________

90 The Value of Tea

91 ______________________________

92 ______________________________

93 ______________________________

94 ______________________________

95 ______________________________

96 ______________________________

97 ______________________________

98 Tea & Clipper Ships

99 ______________________________

100 ______________________________

101 ______________________________

102 ______________________________

103 ______________________________

My Lists

Chinese poet Li Chi Lai during the Song Dynasty said three great evils existed in the land:

1. Bad education of fine youth.
2. Wrongful criticism of fine art.
3. Fine tea wasted through careless brewing.

At-Home Experiences

Tea Flavor ______________________________ Date ____________

Brand ______________________________

Purchased from ______________________________

Price ________ Today's Weather ____________

Brewing Details ______________________________

Who I am with ______________________________

Tea Type: Black
Green
Oolong
White
Herbal
Rooibos
Other

Appearance/Color:

Yellow Yellow–green Green Amber Red Dark brown Black Other

Aroma:

Floral Fruity Citrus Smoky Earthy Grassy Spicy Nutty Chocolate

Faint Moderate Strong Other ____________

Taste:

Floral Fruity Citrus Smoky Earthy Grassy Spicy Nutty Chocolate

Plant/herb Savory Malty Other ______________________________

Delicate Mild Flat Crisp Tangy/tart Sweet Strong

Mouthfeel:

Silky Smooth Brothy Oily Velvety Tingly Brisk Dry Other

My Rating (5 s = best):

Notes

____
____
____
____
____
____
____

At-Home Experiences

Tea Flavor ______________________________ Date ______________

Brand ______________________________

Purchased from ______________________________

Price __________ Today's Weather ______________

Brewing Details ______________________________

Who I am with ______________________________

Tea Type: Black
Green
Oolong
White
Herbal
Rooibos
Other

Appearance/Color:

Yellow Yellow-green Green Amber Red Dark brown Black Other

Aroma:

Floral Fruity Citrus Smoky Earthy Grassy Spicy Nutty Chocolate

Faint Moderate Strong Other ______________________

Taste:

Floral Fruity Citrus Smoky Earthy Grassy Spicy Nutty Chocolate

Plant/herb Savory Malty Other ______________________________

Delicate Mild Flat Crisp Tangy/tart Sweet Strong

Mouthfeel:

Silky Smooth Brothy Oily Velvety Tingly Brisk Dry Other

My Rating (5 🌱s = best): 🌱 🌱 🌱 🌱 🌱

Notes

____

____

____

____

____

____

____

At-Home Experiences

Tea Flavor ______________________ Date ____________

Brand ______________________

Purchased from ______________________

Price ________ Today's Weather ____________

Brewing Details ______________________

Who I am with ______________________

Tea Type: Black
Green
Oolong
White
Herbal
Rooibos
Other

Appearance/Color:

Yellow Yellow-green Green Amber Red Dark brown Black Other

Aroma:

Floral Fruity Citrus Smoky Earthy Grassy Spicy Nutty Chocolate

Faint Moderate Strong Other ____________

Taste:

Floral Fruity Citrus Smoky Earthy Grassy Spicy Nutty Chocolate

Plant/herb Savory Malty Other ____________

Delicate Mild Flat Crisp Tangy/tart Sweet Strong

Mouthfeel:

Silky Smooth Brothy Oily Velvety Tingly Brisk Dry Other

My Rating (5 🌱s = best):

Notes

____

____

____

____

____

____

____

At-Home Experiences

Tea Flavor ______________________________ Date ______________

Brand ______________________________

Purchased from ______________________________

Price ________ Today's Weather ______________

Brewing Details ______________________________

Who I am with ______________________________

Tea Type: Black
Green
Oolong
White
Herbal
Rooibos
Other

Appearance/Color:

Yellow Yellow–green Green Amber Red Dark brown Black Other

Aroma:

Floral Fruity Citrus Smoky Earthy Grassy Spicy Nutty Chocolate

Faint Moderate Strong Other ______________________

Taste:

Floral Fruity Citrus Smoky Earthy Grassy Spicy Nutty Chocolate

Plant/herb Savory Malty Other ______________________________

Delicate Mild Flat Crisp Tangy/tart Sweet Strong

Mouthfeel:

Silky Smooth Brothy Oily Velvety Tingly Brisk Dry Other

My Rating (5 s = best):

Notes

____

____

____

____

____

____

____

Brewing Equipment Guide

Brewing a great cup of tea obviously starts with your choice of tea, but the proper brewing equipment can definitely enhance your experience. Here are some of the basics you'll want to have on hand:

Tea filters: These handy paper sacks come in various sizes, allowing you to essentially make your own tea bag. The difference is they're much larger, providing plenty of room for the leaves to expand.

Infuser basket: Made of stainless steel, plastic or glass, these baskets allow leaves to float freely in your cup without the need for straining. (NOTE: We don't recommend tea balls because they're typically too small to let the leaves float or expand during brewing.)

Fine-mesh strainer: If you choose to brew the leaves directly in the water for fuller flavor, this provides a handy way to keep from having items floating in your cup as you drink. Simply pour from the teapot through the strainer into your cup.

Gaiwan: This three-piece device from China was invented during the Ming dynasty (1368-1644) to brew and serve tea. It consists of a handleless cup, lid and saucer and can be made of glass, porcelain or clay. It's especially good for delicate green or oolong teas – loose leaves are brewed in the cup, then the lid is used to hold back the leaves when pouring.

Teapot: Lots of options here! Cast iron from Japan keeps the tea warm for a long time. Glass is great if you like to watch "the agony of the leaves." Porcelain is often decorated with fancy designs (popular in China and England). Pottery, particularly Yixing from China, takes on the color and taste of tea, so you'll need a separate teapot for each type of tea. (Also keep in mind that you can only rinse and air-dry a clay teapot – never use soap!)

Kettle: Heats the water; both electric and stovetop styles are available.

Tea timer: Use to precisely time the brewing; can be a mini-hourglass or digital (whose beeping helps if you get distracted mid-brewing).

Tea cozy: These are typically made from wool or quilted fabric and are used like a jacket for your teapot to keep it warm longer.

At-Home Experiences

Tea Flavor ______________________________ Date ____________

Brand ______________________________

Purchased from ______________________________

Price ________ Today's Weather ____________

Brewing Details ______________________________

Who I am with ______________________________

Tea Type: Black
Green
Oolong
White
Herbal
Rooibos
Other

Appearance/Color:

Yellow Yellow–green Green Amber Red Dark brown Black Other

Aroma:

Floral Fruity Citrus Smoky Earthy Grassy Spicy Nutty Chocolate

Faint Moderate Strong Other ____________________

Taste:

Floral Fruity Citrus Smoky Earthy Grassy Spicy Nutty Chocolate

Plant/herb Savory Malty Other ____________________

Delicate Mild Flat Crisp Tangy/tart Sweet Strong

Mouthfeel:

Silky Smooth Brothy Oily Velvety Tingly Brisk Dry Other

My Rating (5 's = best):

Notes

____

____

____

____

____

____

____

At-Home Experiences

Tea Flavor ______________________ Date ____________

Brand ______________________

Purchased from ______________________

Price ________ Today's Weather ____________

Brewing Details ______________________

Who I am with ______________________

Tea Type: Black
Green
Oolong
White
Herbal
Rooibos
Other

Appearance/Color:

Yellow Yellow-green Green Amber Red Dark brown Black Other

Aroma:

Floral Fruity Citrus Smoky Earthy Grassy Spicy Nutty Chocolate

Faint Moderate Strong Other ____________

Taste:

Floral Fruity Citrus Smoky Earthy Grassy Spicy Nutty Chocolate

Plant/herb Savory Malty Other ____________

Delicate Mild Flat Crisp Tangy/tart Sweet Strong

Mouthfeel:

Silky Smooth Brothy Oily Velvety Tingly Brisk Dry Other

My Rating (5 s = best):

Notes

At-Home Experiences

Tea Flavor ______________________________ Date ______________

Brand ______________________________

Purchased from ______________________________

Price ________ Today's Weather ______________

Brewing Details ______________________________

Who I am with ______________________________

Tea Type: Black
Green
Oolong
White
Herbal
Rooibos
Other

Appearance/Color:

Yellow Yellow-green Green Amber Red Dark brown Black Other

Aroma:

Floral Fruity Citrus Smoky Earthy Grassy Spicy Nutty Chocolate

Faint Moderate Strong Other ______________________

Taste:

Floral Fruity Citrus Smoky Earthy Grassy Spicy Nutty Chocolate

Plant/herb Savory Malty Other ______________________________

Delicate Mild Flat Crisp Tangy/tart Sweet Strong

Mouthfeel:

Silky Smooth Brothy Oily Velvety Tingly Brisk Dry Other

My Rating (5 s = best):

Notes

____

____

____

____

____

____

____

At-Home Experiences

Tea Flavor ______________________________ Date ____________

Brand ______________________________

Purchased from ______________________________

Price ________ Today's Weather ____________

Brewing Details ______________________________

Who I am with ______________________________

Tea Type: Black
Green
Oolong
White
Herbal
Rooibos
Other

Appearance/Color:

Yellow Yellow–green Green Amber Red Dark brown Black Other

Aroma:

Floral Fruity Citrus Smoky Earthy Grassy Spicy Nutty Chocolate

Faint Moderate Strong Other ____________________

Taste:

Floral Fruity Citrus Smoky Earthy Grassy Spicy Nutty Chocolate

Plant/herb Savory Malty Other ________________________

Delicate Mild Flat Crisp Tangy/tart Sweet Strong

Mouthfeel:

Silky Smooth Brothy Oily Velvety Tingly Brisk Dry Other

My Rating (5 leaves = best):

Notes

____

____

____

____

____

____

____

At-Home Experiences

Tea Flavor ______________________________ Date ____________

Brand ______________________________

Purchased from ______________________________

Price ________ Today's Weather ____________

Brewing Details ______________________________

Who I am with ______________________________

Tea Type: Black
Green
Oolong
White
Herbal
Rooibos
Other

Appearance/Color:

Yellow Yellow-green Green Amber Red Dark brown Black Other

Aroma:

Floral Fruity Citrus Smoky Earthy Grassy Spicy Nutty Chocolate

Faint Moderate Strong Other ____________________

Taste:

Floral Fruity Citrus Smoky Earthy Grassy Spicy Nutty Chocolate

Plant/herb Savory Malty Other ________________________

Delicate Mild Flat Crisp Tangy/tart Sweet Strong

Mouthfeel:

Silky Smooth Brothy Oily Velvety Tingly Brisk Dry Other

My Rating (5 s = best):

Notes

____

____

____

____

____

____

____

Tea Types & Growing Regions

True tea comes from the Camellia sinensis plant, but all teas are certainly not alike! Starting with the least- to most-processed:

White: Once reserved for the Chinese emperor only, these buds with silver-tipped leaves are picked during a very short window of time in the spring. They have a light, delicate flavor and a floral aroma.

Green: Hailing mainly from China, Japan or Korea, these teas are slightly withered, then either pan-fired or steamed and rolled. The pale-colored brew often has a grassy or vegetative taste. The leaves should be brewed at a lower temperature to avoid oversteeping. Popular green teas include: Gunpowder, Hojicha, Genmaicha, Gyokuro, Dragonwell, Sencha and Matcha.

Oolong (or Wu Long): This is one of the most difficult types of tea to produce, since it requires an intricate process of semi-oxidation. Oolongs most often come from China or Taiwan and well-known variations are: Ti quan yin, Silver needle, and White peony. They're good for multiple steepings.

Black: This is probably what most people think of when they hear the word "tea." The leaves are allowed to fully oxidize (wither), giving it a heavy, full-bodied flavor. Most of these teas come from India, China (where they call it "red tea"), or Sri Lanka (formerly Ceylon). Because it is so hearty, black tea is often paired with milk and sugar, especially in Great Britain. Black teas are often named for the region where they're grown: Assam, Darjeeling, Nilgiri, Ceylon, Yunnan, and Keemun. Another well-known variation is Lapsang souchong, which is allowed to oxidize over smoldering pine needles, creating a heavy smoky flavor.

Pu-ehr: You'll often find this fermented tea packed in bricks or disks. It has an earthy taste because it is aged for a very long time. It's produced exclusively in China using a closely-guarded process, and can be very pricey.

Tisane Types & Growing Regions

Although often referred to as tea, these are technically not teas because they contain no leaves from the Camellia sinensis plant. Tisanes can be fruit, floral or herbal infusions (like chamomile, mint, hibiscus, etc.) and are typically caffeine-free.

But the following three tisanes belong in categories of their own:

Rooibos: Grown exclusively in the Cedarberg region of South Africa, this plant (pronounced "roy-boss") is high in vitamin C and antioxidants. (The name means "red bush" in the Afrikaans language.) It has a full-bodied, honey-like flavor and is often blended with fruit or dessert-type flavors. Because it's caffeine-free, it helps to reduce anxiety and promote a good night's sleep, as well as being good for the skin and immune system.

Yerba mate: While only recently popular in the U.S., these leaves from a holly-type plant have been brewed into an everyday beverage in South America for centuries. Pronounced "YUR-bah MAH-tay," it has a strong, vegetal flavor and a natural ability to boost energy without creating the jitters (yes, it does have caffeine). It's grown and enjoyed mainly in Paraguay, Argentina and Brazil, where it is typically brewed in a hollowed-out gourd and drunk with a bombilla (a special straw with a filter on the end).

Guayusa: Similar to yerba mate (although not as grassy or strong), guayusa also comes from a South American holly-type tree. It's grown in a specific region of Ecuador in the Andes Mountains, in the shade of the rainforest on hundreds of small farms. For centuries, the Kichwa people have been drinking this beverage in a daily ceremony that takes place before dawn (around 4 AM) around a communal fire while sharing stories, dreams and songs. In the Kichwa language, this is called being "runa," which means "fully living human being." Guayusa balances the stimulation of caffeine with antioxidant, vitamins and amino acids, which results in making you alert without being anxious or jittery.

At-Home Experiences

Tea Flavor ______________________________ Date ____________

Brand ______________________________

Purchased from ______________________________

Price ________ Today's Weather ____________

Brewing Details ______________________________

Who I am with ______________________________

Tea Type: Black
Green
Oolong
White
Herbal
Rooibos
Other

Appearance/Color:

Yellow Yellow-green Green Amber Red Dark brown Black Other

Aroma:

Floral Fruity Citrus Smoky Earthy Grassy Spicy Nutty Chocolate

Faint Moderate Strong Other ____________________

Taste:

Floral Fruity Citrus Smoky Earthy Grassy Spicy Nutty Chocolate

Plant/herb Savory Malty Other ____________________

Delicate Mild Flat Crisp Tangy/tart Sweet Strong

Mouthfeel:

Silky Smooth Brothy Oily Velvety Tingly Brisk Dry Other

My Rating (5 's = best):

Notes

____

____

____

____

____

____

____

At-Home Experiences

Tea Flavor ______________________________ Date ____________

Brand ______________________________

Purchased from ____________________________

Price ________ Today's Weather ____________

Brewing Details ____________________________

Who I am with ____________________________

Tea Type: Black
Green
Oolong
White
Herbal
Rooibos
Other

Appearance/Color:

Yellow Yellow-green Green Amber Red Dark brown Black Other

Aroma:

Floral Fruity Citrus Smoky Earthy Grassy Spicy Nutty Chocolate

Faint Moderate Strong Other ____________________

Taste:

Floral Fruity Citrus Smoky Earthy Grassy Spicy Nutty Chocolate

Plant/herb Savory Malty Other ________________________

Delicate Mild Flat Crisp Tangy/tart Sweet Strong

Mouthfeel:

Silky Smooth Brothy Oily Velvety Tingly Brisk Dry Other

My Rating (5 🌱s = best): 🌱 🌱 🌱 🌱 🌱

Notes

At-Home Experiences

Tea Flavor ______________________________ Date ____________

Brand ______________________________

Purchased from ______________________________

Price ________ Today's Weather ______________

Brewing Details ______________________________

Who I am with ______________________________

Tea Type: Black
Green
Oolong
White
Herbal
Rooibos
Other

Appearance/Color:

Yellow Yellow–green Green Amber Red Dark brown Black Other

Aroma:

Floral Fruity Citrus Smoky Earthy Grassy Spicy Nutty Chocolate

Faint Moderate Strong Other ______________________

Taste:

Floral Fruity Citrus Smoky Earthy Grassy Spicy Nutty Chocolate

Plant/herb Savory Malty Other ______________________________

Delicate Mild Flat Crisp Tangy/tart Sweet Strong

Mouthfeel:

Silky Smooth Brothy Oily Velvety Tingly Brisk Dry Other

My Rating (5 leaves = best):

Notes

____

____

____

____

____

____

____

At-Home Experiences

Tea Flavor ______________________________ Date ____________

Brand ______________________________

Purchased from ______________________________

Price ________ Today's Weather ____________

Brewing Details ______________________________

Who I am with ______________________________

Tea Type: Black
Green
Oolong
White
Herbal
Rooibos
Other

Appearance/Color:

Yellow Yellow-green Green Amber Red Dark brown Black Other

Aroma:

Floral Fruity Citrus Smoky Earthy Grassy Spicy Nutty Chocolate

Faint Moderate Strong Other ____________________

Taste:

Floral Fruity Citrus Smoky Earthy Grassy Spicy Nutty Chocolate

Plant/herb Savory Malty Other ________________________

Delicate Mild Flat Crisp Tangy/tart Sweet Strong

Mouthfeel:

Silky Smooth Brothy Oily Velvety Tingly Brisk Dry Other

My Rating (5 s = best):

Notes

____

____

____

____

____

____

____

At-Home Experiences

Tea Flavor ______________________________ Date ______________

Brand ______________________________

Purchased from ______________________________

Price ________ Today's Weather ______________

Brewing Details ______________________________

Who I am with ______________________________

Tea Type: Black
Green
Oolong
White
Herbal
Rooibos
Other

Appearance/Color:

Yellow   Yellow-green   Green   Amber   Red   Dark brown   Black   Other

Aroma:

Floral   Fruity   Citrus   Smoky   Earthy   Grassy   Spicy   Nutty   Chocolate

Faint   Moderate   Strong   Other ______________

Taste:

Floral   Fruity   Citrus   Smoky   Earthy   Grassy   Spicy   Nutty   Chocolate

Plant/herb   Savory   Malty   Other ______________

Delicate   Mild   Flat   Crisp   Tangy/tart   Sweet   Strong

Mouthfeel:

Silky   Smooth   Brothy   Oily   Velvety   Tingly   Brisk   Dry   Other

My Rating (5 s = best):

Notes

____

____

____

____

____

____

____

At-Home Experiences

Tea Flavor ______________________ Date ____________

Brand ______________________

Purchased from ______________________

Price ________ Today's Weather ____________

Brewing Details ______________________

Who I am with ______________________

Tea Type: Black
Green
Oolong
White
Herbal
Rooibos
Other

Appearance/Color:

Yellow Yellow–green Green Amber Red Dark brown Black Other

Aroma:

Floral Fruity Citrus Smoky Earthy Grassy Spicy Nutty Chocolate

Faint Moderate Strong Other ______________

Taste:

Floral Fruity Citrus Smoky Earthy Grassy Spicy Nutty Chocolate

Plant/herb Savory Malty Other ______________

Delicate Mild Flat Crisp Tangy/tart Sweet Strong

Mouthfeel:

Silky Smooth Brothy Oily Velvety Tingly Brisk Dry Other

My Rating (5 s = best):

Notes

____

____

____

____

____

____

____

Sweeteners

While some people prefer their tea plain, others choose to sweeten it up a bit. But with what? Here are some of the more common options:

White or granulated sugar: This highly-processed sugar comes from either sugar cane or sugar beets and is easily dissolved.

Raw or turbinado sugar: These chunky, less-processed crystals are the result of spinning cane sugar in a turbine to dry (thus the name), and has a slight molasses flavor. It's not as quick to dissolve.

Brown sugar: White sugar mixed with molasses to give a deeper flavor.

Coconut Palm sugar: Made from the sap of the coconut palm tree; brings out tropical tastes.

Stevia: Made from leaves of the stevia plant and comes in powder or liquid form; contains virtually no calories

Sugar alcohols: These are found naturally in certain fruits. We recommend Erythritol, which is low-glycemic. (Xylitol should be used with caution since it may cause digestive side effects.)

Maple syrup: Comes from the sap of the sugar, red or black maple tree, which is simmered to reduce. The darker it is, the stronger the taste.

Agave nectar: Comes from the pineapple-looking core of the agave plant; has a low glycemic index, but may create a slight vegetal taste.

Honey: Flavors vary, depending on the source (clover, alfalfa, etc.) and tend to bring out floral notes in teas. Raw honey is minimally processed while commercial ones are heated to remove pollen (may also remove health benefits). It's best to find locally-produced honey.

Molasses: This is the syrup left behind during sugar processing. It can range from light to "blackstrap," which is more bitter. It's best only with heavy, earthy teas.

Artificial sweeteners: These include aspartame (often marketed in little blue packets), saccharin (pink packets), and sucralose (yellow packets). While these have no calories, they have been rather controversial over the years and may create an aftertaste.

At-Home Experiences

Tea Flavor ______________________ Date ______________

Brand ______________________

Purchased from ______________________

Price ________ Today's Weather ______________

Brewing Details ______________________

Who I am with ______________________

Tea Type: Black
Green
Oolong
White
Herbal
Rooibos
Other

Appearance/Color:

Yellow Yellow-green Green Amber Red Dark brown Black Other

Aroma:

Floral Fruity Citrus Smoky Earthy Grassy Spicy Nutty Chocolate

Faint Moderate Strong Other ______________

Taste:

Floral Fruity Citrus Smoky Earthy Grassy Spicy Nutty Chocolate

Plant/herb Savory Malty Other ______________

Delicate Mild Flat Crisp Tangy/tart Sweet Strong

Mouthfeel:

Silky Smooth Brothy Oily Velvety Tingly Brisk Dry Other

My Rating (5 s = best): 

Notes

____
____
____
____
____
____
____

At-Home Experiences

Tea Flavor ______________________ Date ____________

Brand ______________________

Purchased from ______________________

Price ________ Today's Weather ____________

Brewing Details ______________________

Who I am with ______________________

Tea Type: Black
Green
Oolong
White
Herbal
Rooibos
Other

Appearance/Color:

Yellow Yellow–green Green Amber Red Dark brown Black Other

Aroma:

Floral Fruity Citrus Smoky Earthy Grassy Spicy Nutty Chocolate

Faint Moderate Strong Other ____________

Taste:

Floral Fruity Citrus Smoky Earthy Grassy Spicy Nutty Chocolate

Plant/herb Savory Malty Other ______________

Delicate Mild Flat Crisp Tangy/tart Sweet Strong

Mouthfeel:

Silky Smooth Brothy Oily Velvety Tingly Brisk Dry Other

My Rating (5 s = best):

Notes

At-Home Experiences

Tea Flavor ______________________________ Date ____________

Brand ______________________________

Purchased from ______________________________

Price ________ Today's Weather ____________

Brewing Details ______________________________

Who I am with ______________________________

Tea Type: Black
Green
Oolong
White
Herbal
Rooibos
Other

Appearance/Color:

Yellow Yellow-green Green Amber Red Dark brown Black Other

Aroma:

Floral Fruity Citrus Smoky Earthy Grassy Spicy Nutty Chocolate

Faint Moderate Strong Other ____________________

Taste:

Floral Fruity Citrus Smoky Earthy Grassy Spicy Nutty Chocolate

Plant/herb Savory Malty Other ______________________________

Delicate Mild Flat Crisp Tangy/tart Sweet Strong

Mouthfeel:

Silky Smooth Brothy Oily Velvety Tingly Brisk Dry Other

My Rating (5 s = best):

Notes

____

____

____

____

____

____

____

At-Home Experiences

Tea Flavor ______________________ Date ____________

Brand ______________________ Tea Type: Black

Purchased from ______________________ Green

Oolong

Price ________ Today's Weather ____________ White

Brewing Details ______________________ Herbal

Rooibos

Who I am with ______________________ Other

Appearance/Color:

Yellow Yellow-green Green Amber Red Dark brown Black Other

Aroma:

Floral Fruity Citrus Smoky Earthy Grassy Spicy Nutty Chocolate

Faint Moderate Strong Other ____________

Taste:

Floral Fruity Citrus Smoky Earthy Grassy Spicy Nutty Chocolate

Plant/herb Savory Malty Other ____________

Delicate Mild Flat Crisp Tangy/tart Sweet Strong

Mouthfeel:

Silky Smooth Brothy Oily Velvety Tingly Brisk Dry Other

My Rating (5 s = best):

Notes

At-Home Experiences

Tea Flavor ______________________________ Date ______________

Brand ______________________________

Purchased from ______________________________

Price ________ Today's Weather ______________

Brewing Details ______________________________

Who I am with ______________________________

Tea Type: Black
Green
Oolong
White
Herbal
Rooibos
Other

Appearance/Color:

Yellow Yellow–green Green Amber Red Dark brown Black Other

Aroma:

Floral Fruity Citrus Smoky Earthy Grassy Spicy Nutty Chocolate

Faint Moderate Strong Other ______________________

Taste:

Floral Fruity Citrus Smoky Earthy Grassy Spicy Nutty Chocolate

Plant/herb Savory Malty Other ______________________________

Delicate Mild Flat Crisp Tangy/tart Sweet Strong

Mouthfeel:

Silky Smooth Brothy Oily Velvety Tingly Brisk Dry Other

My Rating (5 s = best):

Notes

____

____

____

____

____

____

____

The Basics of Cooking with Tea

In many countries, people have used tea as an ingredient in recipes for centuries. We've been cooking with tea at our house for nearly two decades now, and have developed or adapted hundreds of recipes.

Here are some of the basic ways to incorporate tea into your daily meal-planning routine, along with some recipes we've created:

Marinade/Brine: Replace your usual liquid with chosen brewed tea flavor; great for meats of all kinds. (Crème Brûlée Pork, Tea-infused Turkey Breast)

Steaming: Use brewed tea instead of water for vegetables or fish. (Green beans with vanilla tea, Peas with mint tea, etc.)

Soup base: Brewed tea can replace chicken, beef or vegetable stock. (Pumpkin Squash Soup, Coconut Chicken Soup)

Ground as a spice: Measure out a few spoonfuls of loose tea into a spice grinder and pulse until very fine. Then sprinkle the tea into your recipe – chais or smoky teas work especially well. One word of caution: don't try this if your tea contains certain seeds or other ingredients that shouldn't be ground. (Crab-stuffed Tomatoes)

Powder: Mix matcha into ice cream, baked goods, and more.

Blended: Combine your favorite brewed tea in a blender with juices, fruits, and yogurt to make a smoothie.

Reconstitute: Soak dried fruits or veggies in brewed tea. ("Not Your Grandma's Fruitcake")

Substitute for water: Cook rice, pasta or oatmeal in your favorite brewed tea.

(All recipes listed can be found either on the website or in the eMagazine archives found on www.AdventureswithTea.com)

At-Home Experiences

Tea Flavor ______________________ Date ____________

Brand ______________________

Purchased from ______________________

Price ________ Today's Weather ____________

Brewing Details ______________________

Who I am with ______________________

Tea Type: Black
Green
Oolong
White
Herbal
Rooibos
Other

Appearance/Color:

Yellow Yellow-green Green Amber Red Dark brown Black Other

Aroma:

Floral Fruity Citrus Smoky Earthy Grassy Spicy Nutty Chocolate

Faint Moderate Strong Other ____________

Taste:

Floral Fruity Citrus Smoky Earthy Grassy Spicy Nutty Chocolate

Plant/herb Savory Malty Other ____________

Delicate Mild Flat Crisp Tangy/tart Sweet Strong

Mouthfeel:

Silky Smooth Brothy Oily Velvety Tingly Brisk Dry Other

My Rating (5 s = best):

Notes

At-Home Experiences

Tea Flavor ______________________________ Date ______________

Brand ______________________________

Purchased from ______________________________

Price ________ Today's Weather ______________

Brewing Details ______________________________

Who I am with ______________________________

Tea Type: Black
Green
Oolong
White
Herbal
Rooibos
Other

Appearance/Color:

Yellow Yellow-green Green Amber Red Dark brown Black Other

Aroma:

Floral Fruity Citrus Smoky Earthy Grassy Spicy Nutty Chocolate

Faint Moderate Strong Other ______________

Taste:

Floral Fruity Citrus Smoky Earthy Grassy Spicy Nutty Chocolate

Plant/herb Savory Malty Other ______________

Delicate Mild Flat Crisp Tangy/tart Sweet Strong

Mouthfeel:

Silky Smooth Brothy Oily Velvety Tingly Brisk Dry Other

My Rating (5 s = best):

Notes

____

____

____

____

____

____

____

At-Home Experiences

Tea Flavor ______________________ Date ______________

Brand ______________________

Purchased from ______________________

Price ________ Today's Weather ______________

Brewing Details ______________________

Who I am with ______________________

Tea Type: Black
Green
Oolong
White
Herbal
Rooibos
Other

Appearance/Color:

Yellow Yellow–green Green Amber Red Dark brown Black Other

Aroma:

Floral Fruity Citrus Smoky Earthy Grassy Spicy Nutty Chocolate

Faint Moderate Strong Other ______________

Taste:

Floral Fruity Citrus Smoky Earthy Grassy Spicy Nutty Chocolate

Plant/herb Savory Malty Other ______________

Delicate Mild Flat Crisp Tangy/tart Sweet Strong

Mouthfeel:

Silky Smooth Brothy Oily Velvety Tingly Brisk Dry Other

My Rating (5 leaves = best):

Notes

____
____
____
____
____
____
____

At-Home Experiences

Tea Flavor ______________________________ Date ______________

Brand ______________________________

Purchased from ______________________________

Price ________ Today's Weather ______________

Brewing Details ______________________________

Who I am with ______________________________

Tea Type: Black
Green
Oolong
White
Herbal
Rooibos
Other

Appearance/Color:

Yellow Yellow-green Green Amber Red Dark brown Black Other

Aroma:

Floral Fruity Citrus Smoky Earthy Grassy Spicy Nutty Chocolate

Faint Moderate Strong Other ______________

Taste:

Floral Fruity Citrus Smoky Earthy Grassy Spicy Nutty Chocolate

Plant/herb Savory Malty Other ______________

Delicate Mild Flat Crisp Tangy/tart Sweet Strong

Mouthfeel:

Silky Smooth Brothy Oily Velvety Tingly Brisk Dry Other

My Rating (5 s = best):

Notes

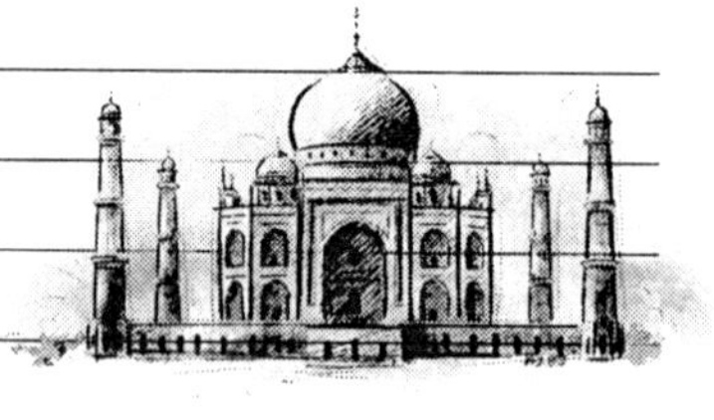

At-Home Experiences

Tea Flavor ______________________ Date ____________

Brand ______________________

Purchased from ______________________

Price ________ Today's Weather ____________

Brewing Details ______________________

Who I am with ______________________

Tea Type: Black
Green
Oolong
White
Herbal
Rooibos
Other

Appearance/Color:

Yellow Yellow–green Green Amber Red Dark brown Black Other

Aroma:

Floral Fruity Citrus Smoky Earthy Grassy Spicy Nutty Chocolate

Faint Moderate Strong Other ______________________

Taste:

Floral Fruity Citrus Smoky Earthy Grassy Spicy Nutty Chocolate

Plant/herb Savory Malty Other ______________________

Delicate Mild Flat Crisp Tangy/tart Sweet Strong

Mouthfeel:

Silky Smooth Brothy Oily Velvety Tingly Brisk Dry Other

My Rating (5 🌱s = best): 🌱 🌱 🌱 🌱 🌱

Notes

____

____

____

____

____

____

____

Tips for Storing Tea

You found a tea you loved, so you bought a pound bag. But over time, you realize it started tasting lifeless and stale. What could you have done differently to keep it tasting fresh longer?

First, don't buy more than you can use within a reasonable amount of time. It's better to buy a small amount of several flavors (4 ounces or less each) and be able to enjoy them all ... but how you store it is important.

Light, heat, air and moisture are the four enemies of processed tea. Keep tea in a pantry, not in a cabinet near the stove or a window. Use a sealed, opaque container. That can be the resealable foil bag it came in, or you can transfer it to an airtight tin. These will keep air and moisture out while the pantry protects it from light and heat.

The worst thing to do is store tea on the counter in a glass jar with a loose lid. When you see condensation or a residue on the inside of the jar as you use it, you've got a problem.

Small portions of tea stored properly can last for months, if not a few years. This gives you the opportunity to choose from all flavors in your pantry and not be limited by the one that's past its prime.

At-Home Experiences

Tea Flavor ______________________________ Date ____________

Brand ______________________________

Purchased from ______________________________

Price __________ Today's Weather ______________

Brewing Details ______________________________

Who I am with ______________________________

Tea Type: Black
Green
Oolong
White
Herbal
Rooibos
Other

Appearance/Color:

Yellow Yellow-green Green Amber Red Dark brown Black Other

Aroma:

Floral Fruity Citrus Smoky Earthy Grassy Spicy Nutty Chocolate

Faint Moderate Strong Other ____________________

Taste:

Floral Fruity Citrus Smoky Earthy Grassy Spicy Nutty Chocolate

Plant/herb Savory Malty Other ____________________

Delicate Mild Flat Crisp Tangy/tart Sweet Strong

Mouthfeel:

Silky Smooth Brothy Oily Velvety Tingly Brisk Dry Other

My Rating (5 leaves = best):

Notes

____

____

____

____

____

____

____

At-Home Experiences

Tea Flavor ______________________ Date ____________

Brand ______________________

Purchased from ______________________

Price ________ Today's Weather ____________

Brewing Details ______________________

Who I am with ______________________

Tea Type: Black
Green
Oolong
White
Herbal
Rooibos
Other

Appearance/Color:

Yellow   Yellow–green   Green   Amber   Red   Dark brown   Black   Other

Aroma:

Floral   Fruity   Citrus   Smoky   Earthy   Grassy   Spicy   Nutty   Chocolate

Faint   Moderate   Strong   Other ____________

Taste:

Floral   Fruity   Citrus   Smoky   Earthy   Grassy   Spicy   Nutty   Chocolate

Plant/herb   Savory   Malty   Other ____________

Delicate   Mild   Flat   Crisp   Tangy/tart   Sweet   Strong

Mouthfeel:

Silky   Smooth   Brothy   Oily   Velvety   Tingly   Brisk   Dry   Other

My Rating (5 s = best):

Notes

At-Home Experiences

Tea Flavor ______________________________ Date ______________

Brand ______________________________

Purchased from ______________________________

Price ________ Today's Weather ______________

Brewing Details ______________________________

Who I am with ______________________________

Tea Type: Black
Green
Oolong
White
Herbal
Rooibos
Other

Appearance/Color:

Yellow Yellow–green Green Amber Red Dark brown Black Other

Aroma:

Floral Fruity Citrus Smoky Earthy Grassy Spicy Nutty Chocolate

Faint Moderate Strong Other ______________________

Taste:

Floral Fruity Citrus Smoky Earthy Grassy Spicy Nutty Chocolate

Plant/herb Savory Malty Other ______________________________

Delicate Mild Flat Crisp Tangy/tart Sweet Strong

Mouthfeel:

Silky Smooth Brothy Oily Velvety Tingly Brisk Dry Other

My Rating (5 s = best):

Notes

____

____

____

____

____

____

____

At-Home Experiences

Tea Flavor ______________________________ Date ____________

Brand ______________________________

Purchased from ______________________________

Price ________ Today's Weather ____________

Brewing Details ______________________________

Who I am with ______________________________

Tea Type: Black
Green
Oolong
White
Herbal
Rooibos
Other

Appearance/Color:

Yellow Yellow–green Green Amber Red Dark brown Black Other

Aroma:

Floral Fruity Citrus Smoky Earthy Grassy Spicy Nutty Chocolate

Faint Moderate Strong Other ____________________

Taste:

Floral Fruity Citrus Smoky Earthy Grassy Spicy Nutty Chocolate

Plant/herb Savory Malty Other ______________________

Delicate Mild Flat Crisp Tangy/tart Sweet Strong

Mouthfeel:

Silky Smooth Brothy Oily Velvety Tingly Brisk Dry Other

My Rating (5 s = best):

Notes

____

____

____

____

____

____

____

At-Home Experiences

Tea Flavor ______________________________ Date ______________

Brand ______________________________

Purchased from ______________________________

Price ________ Today's Weather ______________

Brewing Details ______________________________

Who I am with ______________________________

Tea Type: Black
Green
Oolong
White
Herbal
Rooibos
Other

Appearance/Color:

Yellow Yellow–green Green Amber Red Dark brown Black Other

Aroma:

Floral Fruity Citrus Smoky Earthy Grassy Spicy Nutty Chocolate

Faint Moderate Strong Other ______________

Taste:

Floral Fruity Citrus Smoky Earthy Grassy Spicy Nutty Chocolate

Plant/herb Savory Malty Other ______________

Delicate Mild Flat Crisp Tangy/tart Sweet Strong

Mouthfeel:

Silky Smooth Brothy Oily Velvety Tingly Brisk Dry Other

My Rating (5 s = best):

Notes

____

____

____

____

____

____

____

Beyond the Cup: Other Uses for Tea

The beneficial properties that make tea good for you can also do great things for your skin, hair, and even your home and plants! Check out these ways to use tea that you may not have thought about:

1. Chill a used tea bag* in the fridge for a bit, then use it like a compress for itching or bug bites. (Also good to soothe sunburn.)

2. Soak feet in green or black tea to relieve itching or odor, plus soften skin.

3. Place cooled (and squeezed) bags of tea or rooibos on your eyelids to soothe tired eyes.

4. Brew your favorite tea, then add a bit of honey and lemon to coat and soothe a sore throat.

5. Place a cooled bag of black or green tea on a bruise to stop the spread and help it heal faster.

6. After shampooing, pour a cup of black tea or rooibos over your hair for a nourishing shine. (Use caution if you have blonde hair – you may gain some unexpected highlights!)

7. Soak fabrics or paper in brewed tea for uniquely-dyed creations.

8. Infuse it into your favorite recipes. (Lots of great ideas for you to try on AdventureswithTea.com!)

9. Place dried tea bags inside shoes to control odor.

10. Sprinkle used tea leaves around plants in the garden. (Roses especially love tea!)

*While we typically recommend loose tea over bags (especially the grocery-store bagged teas), you might want to keep some inexpensive bags of tea on hand just for these purposes.

At-Home Experiences

Tea Flavor ______________________________ Date ____________

Brand ______________________________

Purchased from ______________________________

Price ________ Today's Weather ____________

Brewing Details ______________________________

Who I am with ______________________________

Tea Type: Black
Green
Oolong
White
Herbal
Rooibos
Other

Appearance/Color:

Yellow Yellow-green Green Amber Red Dark brown Black Other

Aroma:

Floral Fruity Citrus Smoky Earthy Grassy Spicy Nutty Chocolate

Faint Moderate Strong Other ____________________

Taste:

Floral Fruity Citrus Smoky Earthy Grassy Spicy Nutty Chocolate

Plant/herb Savory Malty Other ______________________________

Delicate Mild Flat Crisp Tangy/tart Sweet Strong

Mouthfeel:

Silky Smooth Brothy Oily Velvety Tingly Brisk Dry Other

My Rating (5 🌱s = best): 🌱 🌱 🌱 🌱 🌱

Notes

____

____

____

____

____

____

____

At-Home Experiences

Tea Flavor ______________________ Date ____________

Brand ______________________

Purchased from ______________________

Price ________ Today's Weather ____________

Brewing Details ______________________

Who I am with ______________________

Tea Type: Black
Green
Oolong
White
Herbal
Rooibos
Other

Appearance/Color:

Yellow Yellow–green Green Amber Red Dark brown Black Other

Aroma:

Floral Fruity Citrus Smoky Earthy Grassy Spicy Nutty Chocolate

Faint Moderate Strong Other ____________

Taste:

Floral Fruity Citrus Smoky Earthy Grassy Spicy Nutty Chocolate

Plant/herb Savory Malty Other ____________

Delicate Mild Flat Crisp Tangy/tart Sweet Strong

Mouthfeel:

Silky Smooth Brothy Oily Velvety Tingly Brisk Dry Other

My Rating (5 s = best):

Notes

At-Home Experiences

Tea Flavor ______________________________ Date ____________

Brand ______________________________ Tea Type: Black

Green

Oolong

White

Herbal

Rooibos

Other

Purchased from ______________________________

Price ________ Today's Weather ____________

Brewing Details ______________________________

Who I am with ______________________________

Appearance/Color:

Yellow Yellow-green Green Amber Red Dark brown Black Other

Aroma:

Floral Fruity Citrus Smoky Earthy Grassy Spicy Nutty Chocolate

Faint Moderate Strong Other ____________________

Taste:

Floral Fruity Citrus Smoky Earthy Grassy Spicy Nutty Chocolate

Plant/herb Savory Malty Other __________________________

Delicate Mild Flat Crisp Tangy/tart Sweet Strong

Mouthfeel:

Silky Smooth Brothy Oily Velvety Tingly Brisk Dry Other

My Rating (5 's = best):

Notes

____

____

____

____

____

____

____

At-Home Experiences

Tea Flavor ______________________________ Date ____________

Brand ______________________________

Purchased from ______________________________

Price ________ Today's Weather ______________

Brewing Details ______________________________

Who I am with ______________________________

Tea Type: Black
Green
Oolong
White
Herbal
Rooibos
Other

Appearance/Color:

Yellow Yellow-green Green Amber Red Dark brown Black Other

Aroma:

Floral Fruity Citrus Smoky Earthy Grassy Spicy Nutty Chocolate

Faint Moderate Strong Other ______________

Taste:

Floral Fruity Citrus Smoky Earthy Grassy Spicy Nutty Chocolate

Plant/herb Savory Malty Other ______________

Delicate Mild Flat Crisp Tangy/tart Sweet Strong

Mouthfeel:

Silky Smooth Brothy Oily Velvety Tingly Brisk Dry Other

My Rating (5 s = best):

Notes

____

____

____

____

____

____

____

At-Home Experiences

Tea Flavor ______________________________ Date ____________

Brand ______________________________

Purchased from ______________________________

Price ________ Today's Weather ____________

Brewing Details ______________________________

Who I am with ______________________________

Tea Type: Black
Green
Oolong
White
Herbal
Rooibos
Other

Appearance/Color:

Yellow Yellow–green Green Amber Red Dark brown Black Other

Aroma:

Floral Fruity Citrus Smoky Earthy Grassy Spicy Nutty Chocolate

Faint Moderate Strong Other ____________________

Taste:

Floral Fruity Citrus Smoky Earthy Grassy Spicy Nutty Chocolate

Plant/herb Savory Malty Other ______________________________

Delicate Mild Flat Crisp Tangy/tart Sweet Strong

Mouthfeel:

Silky Smooth Brothy Oily Velvety Tingly Brisk Dry Other

My Rating (5 leafs = best):

Notes

____

____

____

____

____

____

____

At-Home Experiences

Tea Flavor ______________________________ Date ____________

Brand ______________________________

Purchased from ______________________________

Price ________ Today's Weather ______________

Brewing Details ______________________________

Who I am with ______________________________

Tea Type: Black
Green
Oolong
White
Herbal
Rooibos
Other

Appearance/Color:

Yellow Yellow-green Green Amber Red Dark brown Black Other

Aroma:

Floral Fruity Citrus Smoky Earthy Grassy Spicy Nutty Chocolate

Faint Moderate Strong Other ______________________

Taste:

Floral Fruity Citrus Smoky Earthy Grassy Spicy Nutty Chocolate

Plant/herb Savory Malty Other ______________________________

Delicate Mild Flat Crisp Tangy/tart Sweet Strong

Mouthfeel:

Silky Smooth Brothy Oily Velvety Tingly Brisk Dry Other

My Rating (5 🌱's = best):

Notes

____

____

____

____

____

____

____

At-Home Experiences

Tea Flavor ______________________________ Date ____________

Brand ______________________________

Purchased from ______________________________

Price ________ Today's Weather ______________

Brewing Details ______________________________

Who I am with ______________________________

Tea Type: Black
Green
Oolong
White
Herbal
Rooibos
Other

Appearance/Color:

Yellow Yellow–green Green Amber Red Dark brown Black Other

Aroma:

Floral Fruity Citrus Smoky Earthy Grassy Spicy Nutty Chocolate

Faint Moderate Strong Other ______________________

Taste:

Floral Fruity Citrus Smoky Earthy Grassy Spicy Nutty Chocolate

Plant/herb Savory Malty Other ______________________________

Delicate Mild Flat Crisp Tangy/tart Sweet Strong

Mouthfeel:

Silky Smooth Brothy Oily Velvety Tingly Brisk Dry Other

My Rating (5 s = best):

Notes

A Timeline of Tea History

For centuries, tea has played a major role in the history of countries and cultures around the world. Here are some of the highlights:

2737 B.C.: According to legend, this was when Chinese Emperor Shen Nung first enjoyed tea, after a few leaves fell into his boiling water – back then, it was considered a medicinal drink

618-907 A.D.: During the Tang dynasty in China, tea spread to Japan, planted in Buddhist temple gardens by Japanese monks

780: Chinese poet Lu Yu published **Ch'a Ching (The Classic of Tea)**, a book describing the cultivation, processing and rituals of tea

960-1279: There was a shift from using tea packed in cakes to loose-leaf during the Song dynasty in China; also handcrafted pottery and porcelain teaware became popular

1600: Queen Elizabeth I granted a Royal Charter to create the British East India Company to handle all trade in the East Indies, which led to a 250-year monopoly

1610: Dutch East India Company first brought tea to Europe; it became popular among the rich in the Netherlands, Germany, and France

1618: Tea presented to the Russian Czar, but he rejected it; by 1689, tea was finally exported to Russia via year-long camel caravans to Moscow (continued until the Trans-Siberian Railway opened in 1880)

1650: The Dutch introduce tea in New Amsterdam (today's New York)

1657: Tea served in a London coffee house; it remained a luxury item in England for two centuries

1662: Catherine of Braganza from Portugal married King Charles II of England – she brought tea with her to serve as a court beverage

1773: On December 16, hundreds of chests of tea were dumped into the Boston Harbor in protest of England's tea tax on the American colonies, leading to the American Revolution (prior to that, colonists drank tea daily, but then it became a hated symbol of English power)

1820s: Tea industry introduced in India in an attempt to break from the Chinese monopoly – Scottish adventurer Robert Bruce & his brother Charles were instrumental in the mission

mid-1800s: Anna, Duchess of Bedford, started tradition of "afternoon tea" at 4 p.m.; later, the working class made it into their evening meal

1840s: Clipper ships shaved months off the transportation time for tea from China to arrive in England and the U.S.

1848: British botanist Robert Fortune smuggled tea plants and seeds in his luggage after a trip to China, which were used to launch the tea cultivation in India

1860s: The first tea plants in Ceylon cultivated as a replacement when coffee production began to decline due to disease (by 1890 no coffee plants remained); Scotsman James Taylor was instrumental

1859: Great Atlantic & Pacific Tea Company (later known as A&P) launched in New York (one of several grocery store chains that can trace their history back to tea companies)

1866: Darjeeling had 39 tea gardens; by 1874 there were 113

1869: Suez Canal opened, contributing to end of the clipper ship era

1871: Thomas Lipton opened his first shop in Glasgow; in the 1890s, he bought about 5000 acres of tea estates in Ceylon so he could sell at lower prices in his chain of 300 grocery stores

1903: Tea plants brought from India to Kenya

1904: Iced tea became popular, thanks to Englishman Richard Blechynden serving it at the World's Fair in St. Louis

1908: Tea bags accidentally invented by New York merchant Thomas Sullivan, who sent out loose tea samples in silk bags, but some recipients misunderstood and dropped the bags into their cup. Today, a majority of tea drinkers use bags instead of loose-leaf tea.

1920s: Commercial production of tea bags began in the U.S. (strings and tags were added soon after that)

1928: The first tea from Kenya is sold in London (now that country is third in world production behind China and India)

1960s: Tea bags catch on in Great Britain – today more than 90 percent of the tea served there is in bags

1972: Ceylon officially became Sri Lanka

1987: South Carolina's Charleston Tea Plantation began production

2013: The U.S. League of Tea Growers was formed

Out & About Experiences

Tea Flavor ______________________________ Date ______________

Venue ______________________________

Tea Type: Black
Green
Oolong
White
Herbal
Rooibos
Other

Price ________ Today's Weather ____________

Who I am with ______________________________

My Rating (5 s = best):

Venue
Staff
Tea
Food
Experience

Appearance/Color:

Yellow Yellow-green Green Amber Red Dark brown Black Other

Aroma:

Floral Fruity Citrus Smoky Earthy Grassy Spicy Nutty Chocolate

Faint Moderate Strong Other ____________________

Taste:

Floral Fruity Citrus Smoky Earthy Grassy Spicy Nutty Chocolate

Plant/herb Savory Malty Other ___________________________

Delicate Mild Flat Crisp Tangy/tart Sweet Strong

Mouthfeel:

Silky Smooth Brothy Oily Velvety Tingly Brisk Dry Other

Notes (or attach a business card or memento)

Out & About Experiences

Tea Flavor ______________________________ Date ______________

Venue ______________________________

Price ________ Today's Weather ______________

Who I am with ______________________________

Tea Type: Black
Green
Oolong
White
Herbal
Rooibos
Other

My Rating (5 s = best):

Venue

Staff

Tea

Food

Experience

Appearance/Color:

Yellow Yellow-green Green Amber Red Dark brown Black Other

Aroma:

Floral Fruity Citrus Smoky Earthy Grassy Spicy Nutty Chocolate

Faint Moderate Strong Other ______________________

Taste:

Floral Fruity Citrus Smoky Earthy Grassy Spicy Nutty Chocolate

Plant/herb Savory Malty Other ______________________________

Delicate Mild Flat Crisp Tangy/tart Sweet Strong

Mouthfeel:

Silky Smooth Brothy Oily Velvety Tingly Brisk Dry Other

Notes (or attach a business card or memento)

Out & About Experiences

Tea Flavor ________________________________ Date ______________

Venue ________________________________

Price ________ Today's Weather ______________

Who I am with ________________________________

Tea Type: Black
Green
Oolong
White
Herbal
Rooibos
Other

My Rating (5 s = best):

Venue

Staff

Tea

Food

Experience

Appearance/Color:

Yellow Yellow-green Green Amber Red Dark brown Black Other

Aroma:

Floral Fruity Citrus Smoky Earthy Grassy Spicy Nutty Chocolate

Faint Moderate Strong Other ____________________

Taste:

Floral Fruity Citrus Smoky Earthy Grassy Spicy Nutty Chocolate

Plant/herb Savory Malty Other ____________________

Delicate Mild Flat Crisp Tangy/tart Sweet Strong

Mouthfeel:

Silky Smooth Brothy Oily Velvety Tingly Brisk Dry Other

Notes (or attach a business card or memento)

Out & About Experiences

Tea Flavor ______________________________ Date ____________

Venue ______________________________

Price ________ Today's Weather ____________

Who I am with ______________________________

Tea Type: Black
Green
Oolong
White
Herbal
Rooibos
Other

My Rating (5 leaves = best):

Venue
Staff
Tea
Food
Experience

Appearance/Color:

Yellow Yellow-green Green Amber Red Dark brown Black Other

Aroma:

Floral Fruity Citrus Smoky Earthy Grassy Spicy Nutty Chocolate

Faint Moderate Strong Other __________________

Taste:

Floral Fruity Citrus Smoky Earthy Grassy Spicy Nutty Chocolate

Plant/herb Savory Malty Other ________________________

Delicate Mild Flat Crisp Tangy/tart Sweet Strong

Mouthfeel:

Silky Smooth Brothy Oily Velvety Tingly Brisk Dry Other

Notes (or attach a business card or memento)

Tea in Ancient Medicine

Tea as medicine – that's how it began centuries ago in Asia.

During the Han dynasty (206 B.C. - 221 A.D.), the **Shen Nong's Canon of Herbs** was written. The author states that "if one consumes tea for long enough, the body gains in strength and the mind in keenness."

Huizhong also talks about taking tea for lightness and clarity of mind and the detachment from worldly concerns. Tea is referred to as the elixir of life.

Introducing tea cultivation to Japan, Buddhist monk Eisai wrote in 1211 that "tea is a miraculous medicine for the maintenance of health. Tea has extraordinary power to prolong life. Anywhere a person cultivates tea, long life will follow."

As tea began to make its way across Europe, more people were being introduced to its health benefits. The first European to write about tea was Giambattista Ramusio in a volume of his travels in 1559. He says the people of Szechwan province in China infuse tea in boiling water as a cure for stomach aches and gout.

Of course there has always been controversy about these health benefits. In 1665, German physician Simon Paulli claimed that tea was "... very dangerous to use. It hastens the death of those who drink it, especially if they have passed the age of 40 years."

However, prior to that in 1641 Dutch physician Nikolas Dirx stated: "Nothing is comparable to this plant. Those that use it for that reason, alone, exempt from all maladies and reach extreme old age."

So who are you to believe – helpful or harmful?

Over the years, scientific studies have been conducted on the various health benefits of tea when it comes to digestion, teeth, cancer, cholesterol and more. Tea's polyphenols are front and center because they are antioxidants which can slow down the free radicals that cause cell damage.

Bottom line: Tea is a no-calorie beverage that will keep you hydrated and may benefit you in ways perhaps you never thought about.

Out & About Experiences

Tea Flavor ______________________________ Date ______________

Venue ______________________________

Price ________ Today's Weather ______________

Who I am with ______________________________

Tea Type: Black
Green
Oolong
White
Herbal
Rooibos
Other

My Rating (5 s = best):

Venue

Staff

Tea

Food

Experience

Appearance/Color:

Yellow Yellow–green Green Amber Red Dark brown Black Other

Aroma:

Floral Fruity Citrus Smoky Earthy Grassy Spicy Nutty Chocolate

Faint Moderate Strong Other ______________________

Taste:

Floral Fruity Citrus Smoky Earthy Grassy Spicy Nutty Chocolate

Plant/herb Savory Malty Other ______________________________

Delicate Mild Flat Crisp Tangy/tart Sweet Strong

Mouthfeel:

Silky Smooth Brothy Oily Velvety Tingly Brisk Dry Other

Notes (or attach a business card or memento)

____

____

____

____

____

____

Out & About Experiences

Tea Flavor ______________________________ Date ____________

Venue ______________________________

Price ________ Today's Weather ____________

Who I am with ______________________________

Tea Type: Black
Green
Oolong
White
Herbal
Rooibos
Other

My Rating (5 s = best):

Venue

Staff

Tea

Food

Experience

Appearance/Color:

Yellow Yellow-green Green Amber Red Dark brown Black Other

Aroma:

Floral Fruity Citrus Smoky Earthy Grassy Spicy Nutty Chocolate

Faint Moderate Strong Other ____________________

Taste:

Floral Fruity Citrus Smoky Earthy Grassy Spicy Nutty Chocolate

Plant/herb Savory Malty Other ____________________

Delicate Mild Flat Crisp Tangy/tart Sweet Strong

Mouthfeel:

Silky Smooth Brothy Oily Velvety Tingly Brisk Dry Other

Notes (or attach a business card or memento)

Out & About Experiences

Tea Flavor ______________________________ Date ____________

Venue ______________________________

Price ________ Today's Weather ____________

Who I am with ____________________________

Tea Type: Black, Green, Oolong, White, Herbal, Rooibos, Other

My Rating (5 leaves = best):

Venue
Staff
Tea
Food
Experience

Appearance/Color:

Yellow Yellow-green Green Amber Red Dark brown Black Other

Aroma:

Floral Fruity Citrus Smoky Earthy Grassy Spicy Nutty Chocolate

Faint Moderate Strong Other ____________________

Taste:

Floral Fruity Citrus Smoky Earthy Grassy Spicy Nutty Chocolate

Plant/herb Savory Malty Other ________________________

Delicate Mild Flat Crisp Tangy/tart Sweet Strong

Mouthfeel:

Silky Smooth Brothy Oily Velvety Tingly Brisk Dry Other

Notes (or attach a business card or memento)

Out & About Experiences

Tea Flavor ______________________________ Date ____________

Venue ______________________________

Price ________ Today's Weather ____________

Who I am with ______________________________

Tea Type: Black Green Oolong White Herbal Rooibos Other

My Rating (5 leaves = best):

Venue

Staff

Tea

Food

Experience

Appearance/Color:

Yellow Yellow–green Green Amber Red Dark brown Black Other

Aroma:

Floral Fruity Citrus Smoky Earthy Grassy Spicy Nutty Chocolate

Faint Moderate Strong Other ____________

Taste:

Floral Fruity Citrus Smoky Earthy Grassy Spicy Nutty Chocolate

Plant/herb Savory Malty Other ____________

Delicate Mild Flat Crisp Tangy/tart Sweet Strong

Mouthfeel:

Silky Smooth Brothy Oily Velvety Tingly Brisk Dry Other

Notes (or attach a business card or memento)

Out & About Experiences

Tea Flavor ______________________________ Date ______________

Venue ______________________________

Price ________ Today's Weather ____________

Who I am with ______________________________

Tea Type: Black
Green
Oolong
White
Herbal
Rooibos
Other

My Rating (5 s = best):

Venue

Staff

Tea

Food

Experience

Appearance/Color:

Yellow Yellow–green Green Amber Red Dark brown Black Other

Aroma:

Floral Fruity Citrus Smoky Earthy Grassy Spicy Nutty Chocolate

Faint Moderate Strong Other ____________________

Taste:

Floral Fruity Citrus Smoky Earthy Grassy Spicy Nutty Chocolate

Plant/herb Savory Malty Other ____________________________

Delicate Mild Flat Crisp Tangy/tart Sweet Strong

Mouthfeel:

Silky Smooth Brothy Oily Velvety Tingly Brisk Dry Other

Notes (or attach a business card or memento)

Out & About Experiences

Tea Flavor ______________________________ Date ____________

Venue ______________________________

Price ________ Today's Weather ____________

Who I am with ____________________________

Tea Type: Black
Green
Oolong
White
Herbal
Rooibos
Other

My Rating (5 🌱s = best):

Venue
Staff
Tea
Food
Experience

Appearance/Color:

Yellow Yellow-green Green Amber Red Dark brown Black Other

Aroma:

Floral Fruity Citrus Smoky Earthy Grassy Spicy Nutty Chocolate

Faint Moderate Strong Other ____________________

Taste:

Floral Fruity Citrus Smoky Earthy Grassy Spicy Nutty Chocolate

Plant/herb Savory Malty Other ________________________

Delicate Mild Flat Crisp Tangy/tart Sweet Strong

Mouthfeel:

Silky Smooth Brothy Oily Velvety Tingly Brisk Dry Other

Notes (or attach a business card or memento)

____

____

____

____

____

____

Out & About Experiences

Tea Flavor ______________________________ Date ____________

Venue ______________________________

Price ________ Today's Weather ____________

Who I am with ______________________________

Tea Type: Black
Green
Oolong
White
Herbal
Rooibos
Other

My Rating (5 s = best):

Venue
Staff
Tea
Food
Experience

Appearance/Color:

Yellow Yellow–green Green Amber Red Dark brown Black Other

Aroma:

Floral Fruity Citrus Smoky Earthy Grassy Spicy Nutty Chocolate

Faint Moderate Strong Other ____________________

Taste:

Floral Fruity Citrus Smoky Earthy Grassy Spicy Nutty Chocolate

Plant/herb Savory Malty Other ______________________________

Delicate Mild Flat Crisp Tangy/tart Sweet Strong

Mouthfeel:

Silky Smooth Brothy Oily Velvety Tingly Brisk Dry Other

Notes (or attach a business card or memento)

Who Was Earl Grey?

There are several variations on how the famous tea blend (which is traditionally black tea flavored with oil of the bergamot orange) got its name.

It is most commonly believed that the tea is named after Charles Grey (1764-1845), the 2nd Earl Grey, who served as the British Prime Minister in the 1830s. He was known for the Reform Act of 1832 and the Slavery Abolition Act of 1833.

Some believe that a Chinese mandarin custom-blended the tea as a gift of appreciation to the Earl. But this is curious, since there is no evidence that he ever visited China.

Another version of the story goes that the blend was created by accident when both tea and bergamot oranges were shipped from diplomats in China and the tea absorbed the citrus flavor.

However, **Oxford English Dictionary** researchers have discovered an early reference to bergamot-flavored tea which appeared in 1824, so perhaps none of these versions are reality. (Although the first reference as 'Earl Grey tea' doesn't appear until the 1880s.)

Today there is no one 'Earl Grey' tea, and many companies create their own version of the citrus-scented blend. Some even add cornflower, jasmine or other flowers, and there are also blends made with green tea or rooibos instead of the traditional black teas.

Out & About Experiences

Tea Flavor ______________________________ Date ____________

Venue ______________________________

Price ________ Today's Weather ____________

Who I am with ____________________________

Tea Type: Black
Green
Oolong
White
Herbal
Rooibos
Other

My Rating (5 s = best):

Venue

Staff

Tea

Food

Experience

Appearance/Color:

Yellow Yellow-green Green Amber Red Dark brown Black Other

Aroma:

Floral Fruity Citrus Smoky Earthy Grassy Spicy Nutty Chocolate

Faint Moderate Strong Other ____________________

Taste:

Floral Fruity Citrus Smoky Earthy Grassy Spicy Nutty Chocolate

Plant/herb Savory Malty Other ________________________

Delicate Mild Flat Crisp Tangy/tart Sweet Strong

Mouthfeel:

Silky Smooth Brothy Oily Velvety Tingly Brisk Dry Other

Notes (or attach a business card or memento)

____

____

____

____

____

____

Out & About Experiences

Tea Flavor ______________________________ Date ____________

Venue ______________________________

Price ________ Today's Weather ____________

Who I am with ______________________________

Tea Type: Black
Green
Oolong
White
Herbal
Rooibos
Other

My Rating (5 s = best):

Venue

Staff

Tea

Food

Experience

Appearance/Color:

Yellow Yellow-green Green Amber Red Dark brown Black Other

Aroma:

Floral Fruity Citrus Smoky Earthy Grassy Spicy Nutty Chocolate

Faint Moderate Strong Other ____________________

Taste:

Floral Fruity Citrus Smoky Earthy Grassy Spicy Nutty Chocolate

Plant/herb Savory Malty Other ________________________

Delicate Mild Flat Crisp Tangy/tart Sweet Strong

Mouthfeel:

Silky Smooth Brothy Oily Velvety Tingly Brisk Dry Other

Notes (or attach a business card or memento)

Out & About Experiences

Tea Flavor ______________________________ Date ____________

Venue ______________________________

Price ________ Today's Weather ____________

Who I am with ______________________________

Tea Type: Black, Green, Oolong, White, Herbal, Rooibos, Other

My Rating (5 leaves = best):

- Venue
- Staff
- Tea
- Food
- Experience

Appearance/Color:

Yellow Yellow-green Green Amber Red Dark brown Black Other

Aroma:

Floral Fruity Citrus Smoky Earthy Grassy Spicy Nutty Chocolate

Faint Moderate Strong Other ____________________

Taste:

Floral Fruity Citrus Smoky Earthy Grassy Spicy Nutty Chocolate

Plant/herb Savory Malty Other ______________________________

Delicate Mild Flat Crisp Tangy/tart Sweet Strong

Mouthfeel:

Silky Smooth Brothy Oily Velvety Tingly Brisk Dry Other

Notes (or attach a business card or memento)

Out & About Experiences

Tea Flavor ______________________________ Date ____________

Venue ______________________________

Price ________ Today's Weather ____________

Who I am with ______________________________

Tea Type: Black
Green
Oolong
White
Herbal
Rooibos
Other

My Rating (5 leaves = best):

Venue

Staff

Tea

Food

Experience

Appearance/Color:

Yellow Yellow-green Green Amber Red Dark brown Black Other

Aroma:

Floral Fruity Citrus Smoky Earthy Grassy Spicy Nutty Chocolate

Faint Moderate Strong Other ____________________

Taste:

Floral Fruity Citrus Smoky Earthy Grassy Spicy Nutty Chocolate

Plant/herb Savory Malty Other __________________________

Delicate Mild Flat Crisp Tangy/tart Sweet Strong

Mouthfeel:

Silky Smooth Brothy Oily Velvety Tingly Brisk Dry Other

Notes (or attach a business card or memento)

____

____

____

____

____

____

Out & About Experiences

Tea Flavor ______________________________ Date ______________

Venue ______________________________

Price ________ Today's Weather ______________

Who I am with ______________________________

Tea Type: Black
Green
Oolong
White
Herbal
Rooibos
Other

My Rating (5 🌱s = best):

Venue 🌱🌱🌱🌱🌱

Staff 🌱🌱🌱🌱🌱

Tea 🌱🌱🌱🌱🌱

Food 🌱🌱🌱🌱🌱

Experience 🌱🌱🌱🌱🌱

Appearance/Color:

Yellow Yellow-green Green Amber Red Dark brown Black Other

Aroma:

Floral Fruity Citrus Smoky Earthy Grassy Spicy Nutty Chocolate

Faint Moderate Strong Other ______________

Taste:

Floral Fruity Citrus Smoky Earthy Grassy Spicy Nutty Chocolate

Plant/herb Savory Malty Other ______________

Delicate Mild Flat Crisp Tangy/tart Sweet Strong

Mouthfeel:

Silky Smooth Brothy Oily Velvety Tingly Brisk Dry Other

Notes (or attach a business card or memento)

____

____

____

____

____

____

A History of Afternoon Tea

Today, England is synonymous with tea, but when it was first introduced there in 1657, it was available only to those who could afford the luxury. Even then the English way of tea had a slow start. It took a woman from Portugal to show that tea could be a part of everyday life.

Catherine of Braganza married King Charles II and one of the items she brought with her was tea. Soon it made its way to coffeehouses as an alternative beverage for the men who gathered there (women weren't allowed).

Twinings eventually opened a room where women could come in to drink and purchase tea. It was still very expensive though – three and a half ounces of Chinese gunpowder green tea cost the equivalent of $184 in today's money!

In the 1800s, two very important things happened in the history of English tea. First was the afternoon tea.

At that time, people ate two meals a day, breakfast and a late dinner. Anna, the 7th Duchess of Bedford, would get that feeling of hunger mid-afternoon. She had a pot of tea and a light snack brought to her private room. Over time, she began inviting friends to join her and soon the event moved downstairs to the drawing room.

The second factor was the dramatic drop in prices, making tea affordable for everyone. It became fashionable to have tea and sandwiches in the afternoon about 4 PM.

Soon the middle class joined in with their own version of afternoon tea. High Tea was taken at the dinner table at 6 PM and was considered the day's last meal. So instead of formal rules, crustless sandwiches, and scones, high tea featured pies, meats and cheeses. There were no raised pinkies and it was much more relaxed.

(Excerpted from the Winter 2016 issue of **Adventures with Tea** eMagazine)

Out & About Experiences

Tea Flavor ______________________________ Date ____________

Venue ______________________________

Price ________ Today's Weather ____________

Who I am with ______________________________

Tea Type: Black
Green
Oolong
White
Herbal
Rooibos
Other

My Rating (5 s = best):

Venue

Staff

Tea

Food

Experience

Appearance/Color:

Yellow Yellow–green Green Amber Red Dark brown Black Other

Aroma:

Floral Fruity Citrus Smoky Earthy Grassy Spicy Nutty Chocolate

Faint Moderate Strong Other ____________________

Taste:

Floral Fruity Citrus Smoky Earthy Grassy Spicy Nutty Chocolate

Plant/herb Savory Malty Other ________________________

Delicate Mild Flat Crisp Tangy/tart Sweet Strong

Mouthfeel:

Silky Smooth Brothy Oily Velvety Tingly Brisk Dry Other

Notes (or attach a business card or memento)

Out & About Experiences

Tea Flavor ______________________________ Date ______________

Venue ______________________________

Price ________ Today's Weather ______________

Who I am with ______________________________

Tea Type: Black
Green
Oolong
White
Herbal
Rooibos
Other

My Rating (5 leaves = best):

Venue
Staff
Tea
Food
Experience

Appearance/Color:

Yellow Yellow–green Green Amber Red Dark brown Black Other

Aroma:

Floral Fruity Citrus Smoky Earthy Grassy Spicy Nutty Chocolate

Faint Moderate Strong Other ______________________

Taste:

Floral Fruity Citrus Smoky Earthy Grassy Spicy Nutty Chocolate

Plant/herb Savory Malty Other ______________________________

Delicate Mild Flat Crisp Tangy/tart Sweet Strong

Mouthfeel:

Silky Smooth Brothy Oily Velvety Tingly Brisk Dry Other

Notes (or attach a business card or memento)

Out & About Experiences

Tea Flavor ______________________________ Date ____________

Venue ______________________________

Price ________ Today's Weather ____________

Who I am with ______________________________

Tea Type: Black
Green
Oolong
White
Herbal
Rooibos
Other

My Rating (5 s = best):

Venue

Staff

Tea

Food

Experience

Appearance/Color:

Yellow Yellow-green Green Amber Red Dark brown Black Other

Aroma:

Floral Fruity Citrus Smoky Earthy Grassy Spicy Nutty Chocolate

Faint Moderate Strong Other ____________________

Taste:

Floral Fruity Citrus Smoky Earthy Grassy Spicy Nutty Chocolate

Plant/herb Savory Malty Other ________________________

Delicate Mild Flat Crisp Tangy/tart Sweet Strong

Mouthfeel:

Silky Smooth Brothy Oily Velvety Tingly Brisk Dry Other

Notes (or attach a business card or memento)

____

____

____

____

____

____

Out & About Experiences

Tea Flavor ______________________________ Date ____________

Venue ______________________________ Tea Type: Black

Price ________ Today's Weather ____________ Green

Who I am with ____________________________ Oolong

White

Herbal

Rooibos

Other

My Rating (5 s = best):

Venue

Staff

Tea

Food

Experience

Appearance/Color:

Yellow Yellow-green Green Amber Red Dark brown Black Other

Aroma:

Floral Fruity Citrus Smoky Earthy Grassy Spicy Nutty Chocolate

Faint Moderate Strong Other ____________________

Taste:

Floral Fruity Citrus Smoky Earthy Grassy Spicy Nutty Chocolate

Plant/herb Savory Malty Other __________________________

Delicate Mild Flat Crisp Tangy/tart Sweet Strong

Mouthfeel:

Silky Smooth Brothy Oily Velvety Tingly Brisk Dry Other

Notes (or attach a business card or memento)

Out & About Experiences

Tea Flavor ______________________________ Date ____________

Venue ______________________________

Price ________ Today's Weather ____________

Who I am with ______________________________

Tea Type: Black
Green
Oolong
White
Herbal
Rooibos
Other

My Rating (5 's = best):

Venue
Staff
Tea
Food
Experience

Appearance/Color:

Yellow Yellow–green Green Amber Red Dark brown Black Other

Aroma:

Floral Fruity Citrus Smoky Earthy Grassy Spicy Nutty Chocolate

Faint Moderate Strong Other ____________________

Taste:

Floral Fruity Citrus Smoky Earthy Grassy Spicy Nutty Chocolate

Plant/herb Savory Malty Other ________________________

Delicate Mild Flat Crisp Tangy/tart Sweet Strong

Mouthfeel:

Silky Smooth Brothy Oily Velvety Tingly Brisk Dry Other

Notes (or attach a business card or memento)

____

____

____

____

____

____

Out & About Experiences

Tea Flavor ______________________________ Date ____________

Venue ______________________________

Price ________ Today's Weather ____________

Who I am with ______________________________

Tea Type: Black
Green
Oolong
White
Herbal
Rooibos
Other

My Rating (5 s = best):

Venue

Staff

Tea

Food

Experience

Appearance/Color:

Yellow Yellow-green Green Amber Red Dark brown Black Other

Aroma:

Floral Fruity Citrus Smoky Earthy Grassy Spicy Nutty Chocolate

Faint Moderate Strong Other ____________

Taste:

Floral Fruity Citrus Smoky Earthy Grassy Spicy Nutty Chocolate

Plant/herb Savory Malty Other ______________

Delicate Mild Flat Crisp Tangy/tart Sweet Strong

Mouthfeel:

Silky Smooth Brothy Oily Velvety Tingly Brisk Dry Other

Notes (or attach a business card or memento)

____

____

____

____

____

____

Out & About Experiences

Tea Flavor ______________________________ Date ______________

Venue ______________________________

Price ________ Today's Weather ______________

Who I am with ______________________________

Tea Type: Black
Green
Oolong
White
Herbal
Rooibos
Other

My Rating (5 leaves = best):

Venue
Staff
Tea
Food
Experience

Appearance/Color:

Yellow Yellow-green Green Amber Red Dark brown Black Other

Aroma:

Floral Fruity Citrus Smoky Earthy Grassy Spicy Nutty Chocolate

Faint Moderate Strong Other ______________________

Taste:

Floral Fruity Citrus Smoky Earthy Grassy Spicy Nutty Chocolate

Plant/herb Savory Malty Other ______________________________

Delicate Mild Flat Crisp Tangy/tart Sweet Strong

Mouthfeel:

Silky Smooth Brothy Oily Velvety Tingly Brisk Dry Other

Notes (or attach a business card or memento)

The Value of Tea

Throughout the centuries, tea has launched empires and contributed to the start of wars around the world.

As far back as the Tang dynasty in China (618-907 A.D.), the government began collecting a tea tax. During that time, tea was also used as currency.

China traded bricks of tea to Mongolia in exchange for horses, which became so prevalent that during the Ming dynasty (1368-1677), the Tea and Horse Bureau was established. (It continued up until the early 20th century.) Horses carried up to 130 pounds each.

The Chinese also began trading tea to Russia in exchange for furs, leather and other goods during the 1600s. But that wasn't using horses – camels were the method of transportation for those routes.

When China first began exporting tea to Europe, it was extremely expensive, so only the aristocrats were able to enjoy it. In addition to the high cost, Charles II of England imposed a tax on coffee houses (a primary source for tea) in 1676. By the mid-1700s, tea in England was taxed at 119 percent! So it's no wonder that tea was often smuggled into the country.

Perhaps one reason that tea isn't as popular in the U.S. as in many other countries is due to a long-forgotten tea tax.

The Townshend Acts of 1767 created a tax on a variety of everyday items that the American colonists were allowed to buy exclusively from Britain. After much protest, all those taxes except for tea were repealed in 1770. That led to the famous "Boston Tea Party" in 1773 where more than 300 chests of tea were thrown into the harbor.

Because China held a virtual monopoly on the tea trade, the British began looking for other options around the turn of the 19th century. Thanks to some questionable methods (see more on this in the timeline on pages 62-63), tea is now grown in India and Sri Lanka (formerly Ceylon), as well as other parts of the former British Empire.

Out & About Experiences

Tea Flavor ______________________________ Date ______________

Venue ______________________________

Price ________ Today's Weather ______________

Who I am with ______________________________

Tea Type: Black
Green
Oolong
White
Herbal
Rooibos
Other

My Rating (5 s = best):

Venue

Staff

Tea

Food

Experience

Appearance/Color:

Yellow Yellow-green Green Amber Red Dark brown Black Other

Aroma:

Floral Fruity Citrus Smoky Earthy Grassy Spicy Nutty Chocolate

Faint Moderate Strong Other ____________________

Taste:

Floral Fruity Citrus Smoky Earthy Grassy Spicy Nutty Chocolate

Plant/herb Savory Malty Other ______________________________

Delicate Mild Flat Crisp Tangy/tart Sweet Strong

Mouthfeel:

Silky Smooth Brothy Oily Velvety Tingly Brisk Dry Other

Notes (or attach a business card or memento)

Out & About Experiences

Tea Flavor ______________________________ Date ______________

Venue ______________________________

Price ________ Today's Weather ______________

Who I am with ______________________________

Tea Type: Black

Green

Oolong

White

Herbal

Rooibos

Other

My Rating (5 s = best):

Venue

Staff

Tea

Food

Experience

Appearance/Color:

Yellow Yellow–green Green Amber Red Dark brown Black Other

Aroma:

Floral Fruity Citrus Smoky Earthy Grassy Spicy Nutty Chocolate

Faint Moderate Strong Other ______________________

Taste:

Floral Fruity Citrus Smoky Earthy Grassy Spicy Nutty Chocolate

Plant/herb Savory Malty Other ______________________________

Delicate Mild Flat Crisp Tangy/tart Sweet Strong

Mouthfeel:

Silky Smooth Brothy Oily Velvety Tingly Brisk Dry Other

Notes (or attach a business card or memento)

____

____

____

____

____

____

Out & About Experiences

Tea Flavor ______________________________ Date ____________

Venue ______________________________

Price ________ Today's Weather ____________

Who I am with ______________________________

Tea Type: Black
Green
Oolong
White
Herbal
Rooibos
Other

My Rating (5 s = best):

Venue

Staff

Tea

Food

Experience

Appearance/Color:

Yellow Yellow-green Green Amber Red Dark brown Black Other

Aroma:

Floral Fruity Citrus Smoky Earthy Grassy Spicy Nutty Chocolate

Faint Moderate Strong Other ____________________

Taste:

Floral Fruity Citrus Smoky Earthy Grassy Spicy Nutty Chocolate

Plant/herb Savory Malty Other ________________________

Delicate Mild Flat Crisp Tangy/tart Sweet Strong

Mouthfeel:

Silky Smooth Brothy Oily Velvety Tingly Brisk Dry Other

Notes (or attach a business card or memento)

____

____

____

____

____

____

Out & About Experiences

Tea Flavor ______________________________ Date ____________

Venue ______________________________

Price ________ Today's Weather ____________

Who I am with ______________________________

My Rating (5 leaves = best):

Venue

Staff

Tea

Food

Experience

Tea Type: Black

Green

Oolong

White

Herbal

Rooibos

Other

Appearance/Color:

Yellow Yellow-green Green Amber Red Dark brown Black Other

Aroma:

Floral Fruity Citrus Smoky Earthy Grassy Spicy Nutty Chocolate

Faint Moderate Strong Other ____________

Taste:

Floral Fruity Citrus Smoky Earthy Grassy Spicy Nutty Chocolate

Plant/herb Savory Malty Other ____________

Delicate Mild Flat Crisp Tangy/tart Sweet Strong

Mouthfeel:

Silky Smooth Brothy Oily Velvety Tingly Brisk Dry Other

Notes (or attach a business card or memento)

Out & About Experiences

Tea Flavor ______________________________ Date ______________

Venue ______________________________

Price ________ Today's Weather ______________

Who I am with ______________________________

Tea Type: Black
Green
Oolong
White
Herbal
Rooibos
Other

My Rating (5 s = best):

- Venue
- Staff
- Tea
- Food
- Experience

Appearance/Color:

Yellow Yellow-green Green Amber Red Dark brown Black Other

Aroma:

Floral Fruity Citrus Smoky Earthy Grassy Spicy Nutty Chocolate

Faint Moderate Strong Other ______________________

Taste:

Floral Fruity Citrus Smoky Earthy Grassy Spicy Nutty Chocolate

Plant/herb Savory Malty Other ______________________________

Delicate Mild Flat Crisp Tangy/tart Sweet Strong

Mouthfeel:

Silky Smooth Brothy Oily Velvety Tingly Brisk Dry Other

Notes (or attach a business card or memento)

____

____

____

____

____

____

Out & About Experiences

Tea Flavor ______________________________ Date ______________

Venue ______________________________

Price ________ Today's Weather ____________

Who I am with ______________________________

Tea Type: Black
Green
Oolong
White
Herbal
Rooibos
Other

My Rating (5 s = best):

Venue

Staff

Tea

Food

Experience

Appearance/Color:

Yellow Yellow-green Green Amber Red Dark brown Black Other

Aroma:

Floral Fruity Citrus Smoky Earthy Grassy Spicy Nutty Chocolate

Faint Moderate Strong Other ______________

Taste:

Floral Fruity Citrus Smoky Earthy Grassy Spicy Nutty Chocolate

Plant/herb Savory Malty Other ______________

Delicate Mild Flat Crisp Tangy/tart Sweet Strong

Mouthfeel:

Silky Smooth Brothy Oily Velvety Tingly Brisk Dry Other

Notes (or attach a business card or memento)

Out & About Experiences

Tea Flavor ______________________________ Date ____________

Venue ______________________________

Price ________ Today's Weather ____________

Who I am with ______________________________

Tea Type: Black
Green
Oolong
White
Herbal
Rooibos
Other

My Rating (5 s = best):

Venue

Staff

Tea

Food

Experience

Appearance/Color:

Yellow Yellow-green Green Amber Red Dark brown Black Other

Aroma:

Floral Fruity Citrus Smoky Earthy Grassy Spicy Nutty Chocolate

Faint Moderate Strong Other ____________________

Taste:

Floral Fruity Citrus Smoky Earthy Grassy Spicy Nutty Chocolate

Plant/herb Savory Malty Other ______________________________

Delicate Mild Flat Crisp Tangy/tart Sweet Strong

Mouthfeel:

Silky Smooth Brothy Oily Velvety Tingly Brisk Dry Other

Notes (or attach a business card or memento)

____

____

____

____

____

____

Tea & Clipper Ships

As tea gained popularity during the early 1800s, transporting it from the plantations in Asia to the shops in Europe and the Americas was a constant challenge.

Ships were of course the best option, but travel was extremely slow – about 150 miles per day or less. So to go from China to London or America took an extremely long time.

Then in the 1830s and 40s, a new style of merchant ship emerged. Long and narrow, they were much faster with three masts and a square rig. They didn't push through the waves, they clipped over them. With a focus on speed, they had limited cargo space.

In 1843, clipper ships entered their boom years of bringing tea from China. They sailed all over the world, but mostly on the standard trade routes.

There were competitions – actual races for who could deliver fresh tea the fastest. A world record was set by the Flying Cloud in 1854. It sailed from New York around South America to San Francisco in 89 days and eight hours – a record that held for more than a century, until 1989.

In a dramatic finish during the Great Tea Race of 1866, two ships arrived in London within minutes of each other after 99 days at sea, so the Ariel and Taeping split the prize money.

One of the last clipper ships built was the Cutty Sark. She is now dry-docked on display in England. The era of the clipper came to a close with the dawn of more powerful steam ships and the opening of the Suez Canal in 1869.

Illustration by Pearson Scott Foresman [Public domain], via Wikimedia Commons

Out & About Experiences

Tea Flavor ______________________________ Date ____________

Venue ______________________________

Price ________ Today's Weather ____________

Who I am with ______________________________

Tea Type: Black
Green
Oolong
White
Herbal
Rooibos
Other

My Rating (5 's = best):

Venue

Staff

Tea

Food

Experience

Appearance/Color:

Yellow Yellow–green Green Amber Red Dark brown Black Other

Aroma:

Floral Fruity Citrus Smoky Earthy Grassy Spicy Nutty Chocolate

Faint Moderate Strong Other ____________________

Taste:

Floral Fruity Citrus Smoky Earthy Grassy Spicy Nutty Chocolate

Plant/herb Savory Malty Other ________________________

Delicate Mild Flat Crisp Tangy/tart Sweet Strong

Mouthfeel:

Silky Smooth Brothy Oily Velvety Tingly Brisk Dry Other

Notes (or attach a business card or memento)

____

____

____

____

____

____

Out & About Experiences

Tea Flavor ______________________________ Date ____________

Venue ______________________________ Tea Type: Black

Price ________ Today's Weather ____________ Green

Who I am with ______________________________ Oolong

White

Herbal

Rooibos

Other

My Rating (5 s = best):

Venue

Staff

Tea

Food

Experience

Appearance/Color:

Yellow Yellow-green Green Amber Red Dark brown Black Other

Aroma:

Floral Fruity Citrus Smoky Earthy Grassy Spicy Nutty Chocolate

Faint Moderate Strong Other ____________________

Taste:

Floral Fruity Citrus Smoky Earthy Grassy Spicy Nutty Chocolate

Plant/herb Savory Malty Other ________________________

Delicate Mild Flat Crisp Tangy/tart Sweet Strong

Mouthfeel:

Silky Smooth Brothy Oily Velvety Tingly Brisk Dry Other

Notes (or attach a business card or memento)

____

____

____

____

____

____

Out & About Experiences

Tea Flavor ______________________________ Date ____________

Venue ______________________________

Price ________ Today's Weather ____________

Who I am with ______________________________

Tea Type: Black
Green
Oolong
White
Herbal
Rooibos
Other

My Rating (5 s = best):

Venue

Staff

Tea

Food

Experience

Appearance/Color:

Yellow Yellow-green Green Amber Red Dark brown Black Other

Aroma:

Floral Fruity Citrus Smoky Earthy Grassy Spicy Nutty Chocolate

Faint Moderate Strong Other ____________________

Taste:

Floral Fruity Citrus Smoky Earthy Grassy Spicy Nutty Chocolate

Plant/herb Savory Malty Other ____________________________

Delicate Mild Flat Crisp Tangy/tart Sweet Strong

Mouthfeel:

Silky Smooth Brothy Oily Velvety Tingly Brisk Dry Other

Notes (or attach a business card or memento)

____

____

____

____

____

____

Out & About Experiences

Tea Flavor ______________________________ Date ______________

Venue ______________________________

Price ________ Today's Weather ____________

Who I am with ______________________________

Tea Type: Black
Green
Oolong
White
Herbal
Rooibos
Other

My Rating (5 s = best):

Venue

Staff

Tea

Food

Experience

Appearance/Color:

Yellow Yellow–green Green Amber Red Dark brown Black Other

Aroma:

Floral Fruity Citrus Smoky Earthy Grassy Spicy Nutty Chocolate

Faint Moderate Strong Other ____________________

Taste:

Floral Fruity Citrus Smoky Earthy Grassy Spicy Nutty Chocolate

Plant/herb Savory Malty Other __________________________

Delicate Mild Flat Crisp Tangy/tart Sweet Strong

Mouthfeel:

Silky Smooth Brothy Oily Velvety Tingly Brisk Dry Other

Notes (or attach a business card or memento)

Out & About Experiences

Tea Flavor ______________________________ Date ____________

Venue ______________________________ Tea Type: Black

Price ________ Today's Weather ____________ Green

Who I am with ______________________________ Oolong

White

My Rating (5 s = best): Herbal

Venue Rooibos

Staff Other

Tea

Food

Experience

Appearance/Color:

Yellow Yellow-green Green Amber Red Dark brown Black Other

Aroma:

Floral Fruity Citrus Smoky Earthy Grassy Spicy Nutty Chocolate

Faint Moderate Strong Other ____________________

Taste:

Floral Fruity Citrus Smoky Earthy Grassy Spicy Nutty Chocolate

Plant/herb Savory Malty Other __________________________

Delicate Mild Flat Crisp Tangy/tart Sweet Strong

Mouthfeel:

Silky Smooth Brothy Oily Velvety Tingly Brisk Dry Other

Notes (or attach a business card or memento)

____

____

____

____

____

____

Tea Types & Blends

You'll find the following tea type and blend names going either forwards or backwards in any direction:

Black	Tisane	Guayusa
Green	Herbal	English Breakfast
Oolong	Chai	Earl Grey
White	Rooibos	
Pu-erh	Yerba mate	

R	T	M	Q	T	R	Y	Z	Q	M	G	B	Q	X	P	N	D
O	L	S	N	K	Y	D	Y	N	T	T	R	P	D	D	M	V
O	Z	M	A	X	Q	L	L	N	X	Q	Q	Y	N	N	P	Q
I	T	B	Z	F	L	A	B	R	E	H	D	B	L	X	L	X
B	Z	D	M	J	K	N	L	J	M	B	P	N	B	T	Z	Z
O	X	B	Z	N	Q	A	P	Y	J	U	E	Y	E	Z	R	V
S	D	Q	B	G	T	Y	E	N	E	T	R	A	B	E	X	Y
Y	E	R	G	L	R	A	E	R	A	D	S	N	M	N	R	J
V	P	W	W	R	A	X	H	M	B	U	O	O	L	O	N	G
E	W	W	R	L	X	C	A	Z	Y	H	E	D	W	Y	T	T
L	N	N	B	W	T	B	K	A	L	T	S	T	R	L	B	T
N	J	A	K	K	R	J	U	J	D	Z	X	I	I	Q	C	W
Z	V	M	S	E	T	G	V	M	L	L	Z	J	L	H	M	N
X	L	Y	Y	I	B	Z	T	P	K	D	B	M	A	G	W	G
K	X	Z	R	D	T	L	L	Z	L	J	W	I	J	P	N	V
Q	R	P	G	R	B	Q	L	T	J	J	K	P	M	K	W	E

(Puzzle made at puzzle-maker.com)

Out & About Experiences

Tea Flavor ______________________________ Date ______________

Venue ______________________________ Tea Type: Black

Price ________ Today's Weather ______________ Green

Who I am with ______________________________ Oolong

White

My Rating (5 s = best): Herbal

Venue Rooibos

Staff Other

Tea

Food

Experience

Appearance/Color:

Yellow Yellow–green Green Amber Red Dark brown Black Other

Aroma:

Floral Fruity Citrus Smoky Earthy Grassy Spicy Nutty Chocolate

Faint Moderate Strong Other ____________________

Taste:

Floral Fruity Citrus Smoky Earthy Grassy Spicy Nutty Chocolate

Plant/herb Savory Malty Other __________________________

Delicate Mild Flat Crisp Tangy/tart Sweet Strong

Mouthfeel:

Silky Smooth Brothy Oily Velvety Tingly Brisk Dry Other

Notes (or attach a business card or memento)

Out & About Experiences

Tea Flavor ______________________ Date ____________

Venue ______________________

Price ________ Today's Weather ____________

Who I am with ______________________

Tea Type: Black
Green
Oolong
White
Herbal
Rooibos
Other

My Rating (5 s = best):

Venue
Staff
Tea
Food
Experience

Appearance/Color:

Yellow Yellow-green Green Amber Red Dark brown Black Other

Aroma:

Floral Fruity Citrus Smoky Earthy Grassy Spicy Nutty Chocolate

Faint Moderate Strong Other ____________

Taste:

Floral Fruity Citrus Smoky Earthy Grassy Spicy Nutty Chocolate

Plant/herb Savory Malty Other ____________

Delicate Mild Flat Crisp Tangy/tart Sweet Strong

Mouthfeel:

Silky Smooth Brothy Oily Velvety Tingly Brisk Dry Other

Notes (or attach a business card or memento)

Out & About Experiences

Tea Flavor ____________________________ Date ______________

Venue ____________________________

Price ________ Today's Weather ______________

Who I am with ____________________________

Tea Type: Black
Green
Oolong
White
Herbal
Rooibos
Other

My Rating (5 leaves = best):

Venue
Staff
Tea
Food
Experience

Appearance/Color:

Yellow Yellow–green Green Amber Red Dark brown Black Other

Aroma:

Floral Fruity Citrus Smoky Earthy Grassy Spicy Nutty Chocolate

Faint Moderate Strong Other ______________

Taste:

Floral Fruity Citrus Smoky Earthy Grassy Spicy Nutty Chocolate

Plant/herb Savory Malty Other ______________

Delicate Mild Flat Crisp Tangy/tart Sweet Strong

Mouthfeel:

Silky Smooth Brothy Oily Velvety Tingly Brisk Dry Other

Notes (or attach a business card or memento)

Out & About Experiences

Tea Flavor ______________________________ Date ____________

Venue ______________________________

Tea Type: Black
Green
Oolong
White
Herbal
Rooibos
Other

Price ________ Today's Weather ____________

Who I am with ______________________________

My Rating (5 s = best):

Venue
Staff
Tea
Food
Experience

Appearance/Color:

Yellow Yellow-green Green Amber Red Dark brown Black Other

Aroma:

Floral Fruity Citrus Smoky Earthy Grassy Spicy Nutty Chocolate

Faint Moderate Strong Other ________________

Taste:

Floral Fruity Citrus Smoky Earthy Grassy Spicy Nutty Chocolate

Plant/herb Savory Malty Other ________________________

Delicate Mild Flat Crisp Tangy/tart Sweet Strong

Mouthfeel:

Silky Smooth Brothy Oily Velvety Tingly Brisk Dry Other

Notes (or attach a business card or memento)

Out & About Experiences

Tea Flavor ______________________________ Date ____________

Venue ______________________________

Price ________ Today's Weather ____________

Who I am with ______________________________

Tea Type: Black
Green
Oolong
White
Herbal
Rooibos
Other

My Rating (5 leaves = best):

Venue

Staff

Tea

Food

Experience

Appearance/Color:

Yellow Yellow–green Green Amber Red Dark brown Black Other

Aroma:

Floral Fruity Citrus Smoky Earthy Grassy Spicy Nutty Chocolate

Faint Moderate Strong Other ____________________

Taste:

Floral Fruity Citrus Smoky Earthy Grassy Spicy Nutty Chocolate

Plant/herb Savory Malty Other ________________________

Delicate Mild Flat Crisp Tangy/tart Sweet Strong

Mouthfeel:

Silky Smooth Brothy Oily Velvety Tingly Brisk Dry Other

Notes (or attach a business card or memento)

____

____

____

____

____

____

Tea & Tisane Growing Regions

You'll find the following tea and tisane growing region names going either forwards or backwards in any direction:

India	Korea	Darjeeling	South Africa
China	Sri Lanka	Nilgiri	Brazil
Japan	Kenya	Yunnan	Argentina
Taiwan	Assam	Keemun	Ecuador

S	A	S	S	A	M	T	R	Y	B	L	W	Z	D
A	O	L	Z	M	P	Z	D	B	B	W	B	Z	M
N	N	U	M	G	T	M	D	T	W	Y	Y	Y	R
I	J	I	T	D	A	R	J	E	E	L	I	N	G
L	M	T	T	H	A	K	N	A	L	I	R	S	B
G	R	X	B	N	A	K	A	D	B	W	J	N	T
I	K	O	Z	R	E	F	R	N	K	N	A	T	M
R	E	P	D	N	A	G	R	O	I	W	G	N	L
I	E	J	Y	A	I	Z	R	I	I	H	A	L	B
Z	M	A	A	N	U	E	I	A	C	N	C	W	B
Z	U	Y	D	P	A	C	T	L	N	A	Z	Y	Y
Y	N	I	J	M	A	Y	E	U	N	M	Z	R	G
V	A	B	B	M	R	N	Y	R	W	D	G	D	T

(Puzzle made at puzzle-maker.com)

Out & About Experiences

Tea Flavor ____________________________ Date ______________

Venue ____________________________

Price ________ Today's Weather ______________

Who I am with ____________________________

Tea Type: Black
Green
Oolong
White
Herbal
Rooibos
Other

My Rating (5 s = best):

Venue

Staff

Tea

Food

Experience

Appearance/Color:

Yellow Yellow-green Green Amber Red Dark brown Black Other

Aroma:

Floral Fruity Citrus Smoky Earthy Grassy Spicy Nutty Chocolate

Faint Moderate Strong Other ______________________

Taste:

Floral Fruity Citrus Smoky Earthy Grassy Spicy Nutty Chocolate

Plant/herb Savory Malty Other ____________________________

Delicate Mild Flat Crisp Tangy/tart Sweet Strong

Mouthfeel:

Silky Smooth Brothy Oily Velvety Tingly Brisk Dry Other

Notes (or attach a business card or memento)

____

____

____

____

____

____

Out & About Experiences

Tea Flavor ______________________________ Date ____________

Venue ______________________________

Price ________ Today's Weather ____________

Who I am with ______________________________

Tea Type: Black Green Oolong White Herbal Rooibos Other

My Rating (5 s = best):

Venue

Staff

Tea

Food

Experience

Appearance/Color:

Yellow Yellow-green Green Amber Red Dark brown Black Other

Aroma:

Floral Fruity Citrus Smoky Earthy Grassy Spicy Nutty Chocolate

Faint Moderate Strong Other ____________________

Taste:

Floral Fruity Citrus Smoky Earthy Grassy Spicy Nutty Chocolate

Plant/herb Savory Malty Other ________________________

Delicate Mild Flat Crisp Tangy/tart Sweet Strong

Mouthfeel:

Silky Smooth Brothy Oily Velvety Tingly Brisk Dry Other

Notes (or attach a business card or memento)

Out & About Experiences

Tea Flavor ______________________________ Date ____________

Venue ______________________________

Price ________ Today's Weather ____________

Who I am with ______________________________

Tea Type: Black
Green
Oolong
White
Herbal
Rooibos
Other

My Rating (5 's = best):

Venue

Staff

Tea

Food

Experience

Appearance/Color:

Yellow Yellow–green Green Amber Red Dark brown Black Other

Aroma:

Floral Fruity Citrus Smoky Earthy Grassy Spicy Nutty Chocolate

Faint Moderate Strong Other ____________________

Taste:

Floral Fruity Citrus Smoky Earthy Grassy Spicy Nutty Chocolate

Plant/herb Savory Malty Other ________________________

Delicate Mild Flat Crisp Tangy/tart Sweet Strong

Mouthfeel:

Silky Smooth Brothy Oily Velvety Tingly Brisk Dry Other

Notes (or attach a business card or memento)

Out & About Experiences

Tea Flavor ______________________ Date __________

Venue ______________________

Tea Type: Black / Green / Oolong / White / Herbal / Rooibos / Other

Price ________ Today's Weather __________

Who I am with ______________________

My Rating (5 🌱s = best):

Venue

Staff

Tea

Food

Experience

Appearance/Color:

Yellow Yellow–green Green Amber Red Dark brown Black Other

Aroma:

Floral Fruity Citrus Smoky Earthy Grassy Spicy Nutty Chocolate

Faint Moderate Strong Other __________

Taste:

Floral Fruity Citrus Smoky Earthy Grassy Spicy Nutty Chocolate

Plant/herb Savory Malty Other __________

Delicate Mild Flat Crisp Tangy/tart Sweet Strong

Mouthfeel:

Silky Smooth Brothy Oily Velvety Tingly Brisk Dry Other

Notes (or attach a business card or memento)

Places I Want to Visit

People I Want to Share Tea With

Types of Tea I Want to Try

About the Authors

Alan Arnold spent more than 12 years as a barista and café manager in Kansas City, making more than a half-million drinks. While much of that was coffee, he always had a passion for tea, and one year was number three in the U.S. for tea sales (out of more than 600 cafés).

After losing his job in 2009, he and his wife, Marlys, set out to fulfill his dream of having a private line of tea. They chose the name **Adventures with Tea** to emphasize that it doesn't have to be like the plain, boring tea people may remember from Grandma's house ... tea can be fun and funky, in addition to being tasty and healthy.

But the couple doesn't stop at promoting tea as a beverage. They also use it as a recipe ingredient in everything from main dishes to desserts. Over the past two decades, they've developed hundreds of tea-infused recipes, which they share in cooking classes as well as in their own eMagazine. Many of those recipes are also published on their blog.

Connect with Alan & Marlys:

www.AdventureswithTea.com
Facebook: @AdventureswithTea
Twitter: @adv_tea
YouTube: @AdventureswithTea

More from the Authors:

Adventures with Tea
eMagazine archives

Blog featuring
tea-infused recipes

Gourmet
loose-leaf teas

Learn more at: www.AdventureswithTea.com

CPSIA information can be obtained
at www.ICGtesting.com
Printed in the USA
FFOW04n1709101117
43393686-42036FF

9 780971 290556